POKÉMON™

ADVENTURES

RUBY & SAPPHIRE

D0461857

**Pokémon ADVENTURES
Ruby and Sapphire**
Volume 17
VIZ Media Edition

**Story by HIDENORI KUSAKA
Art by SATOSHI YAMAMOTO**

© 2013 Pokémon.
© 1995–2004 Nintendo / Creatures Inc. / GAME FREAK inc.
TM, ®, and character names are trademarks of Nintendo.
POCKET MONSTERS SPECIAL Vol. 17
by Hidenori KUSAKA, Satoshi YAMAMOTO
© 1997 Hidenori KUSAKA, Satoshi YAMAMOTO
All rights reserved.
Original Japanese edition published by SHOGAKUKAN.
English translation rights in the United States of America, Canada,
the United Kingdom, Ireland, Australia, New Zealand and India arranged with SHOGAKUKAN.

English Adaptation/Bryant Turnage
Translation/Tetsuichiro Miyaki
Touch-up & Lettering/Annaliese Christman
Design/Shawn Carrico
Editor/Annette Roman

The stories, characters and incidents mentioned
in this publication are entirely fictional.

No portion of this book may be reproduced or transmitted in
any form or by any means without written permission from
the copyright holders.

Printed in the U.S.A.

Published by VIZ Media, LLC
P.O. Box 77010
San Francisco, CA 94107

10 9 8 7
First printing, July 2013
Seventh printing, June 2020

viz.com

PARENTAL ADVISORY
POKÉMON ADVENTURES is rated A
and is suitable for readers of all ages.

POKÉMON

ADVENTURES
RUBY & SAPPHIRE

17
VOLUME SEVENTEEN

Story by
Hidenori Kusaka

Art by
Satoshi Yamamoto

Sapphire

Professor Birch

A Hoenn region Pokémon researcher.

Our Story So Far...

Some place in some time... in the Hoenn region. A young boy named Ruby moves to Hoenn from Johto. His dream? To become the champion of Pokémon Contests, competitions in which Pokémon are compared in terms of their coolness, beauty, cuteness, smartness and toughness! Unable to handle the pressure from his father—new Hoenn Gym Leader Norman—to fight Pokémon battles, Ruby runs away from home. Thus begins his exploration of the vast Hoenn region...

Ruby

Amber

Archie's most trusted follower. He has a Carvanha.

Shelly

A member of Team Aqua who has a Ludicolo.

Matt

One of three members of the Team Aqua SSS. Muscular and intelligent.

Archie

The leader of mysterious Team Aqua. A ruthless, cold-hearted man.

Ty

Gabby's trusty
camera operator.

Gabby

A busybody
Hoenn TV reporter.

Steven

A mysterious
Trainer Ruby met
near Dewford Town.

Norman

Ruby's father, the
Gym Leader of
Petalburg City.

Ruby meets a girl named Sapphire
who lives in a cave. Like Ruby,
she has a dream. Hers is to
defeat all the Gym Leaders in
the Hoenn region. The two agree
to pursue their dreams for 80
days, then reunite at the spot
where they first met. And thus,
Ruby and Sapphire's 80-day
journey through Hoenn begins.

Sapphire successfully defeats the
Gym Leaders of two Pokémon Gyms
and hurries towards her third Gym.
Meanwhile, Ruby is captured by Team
Magma at Slateport City, but manages
to escape inside Submarine Explorer 1.
Unfortunately, now he must face Blaise
inside the sinking submarine!

Blaise

One of the Three
Fires of Team Magma.
Ruby must battle him
in Explorer 1.

Courtney

The only female of the
Three Fires of Team
Magma. Fiesty and a
skilled tactician.

Tabitha

One of the Three
Fires of Team Magma.
He has a Torkoal.

Maxie

The leader of
Team Magma.

SAPPHIRE

TRAINERS OF THE FOURTH CHAPTER

RUBY

SAPPHIRE ● AGE 10

Sapphire grew up partly feral in the wilderness. She has learned to channel the powers of nature. Her dream is to defeat every single Gym Leader in the Hoenn region!!

RUBY ● AGE 11

A young boy who just moved to the Hoenn region from Johto. He loves Pokémon Contests and has zero interest in Pokémon battling. But does he secretly have a talent for it...?

CHIC
COMBUSKEN ♀
Introverted. Uses fire-type moves.

NANA
MIGHTYENA ♀
Naive. Represents Cuteness.

RONO
LAIRON ♂
Mischievous. Proud of his toughness.

KIKI
DELCATTY ♀
Intense. Represents Coolness.

LORRY
WAILORD ♂
Bold. Sapphire rides him across seas.

MUMU
MARSHTOMP ♂
Easygoing. Represents Toughness?

POKÉMON
ADVENTURES
RUBY & SAPPHIRE

17
VOLUME SEVENTEEN

CONTENTS

● Chapter 202 ●
Slugging It Out with Slugma II

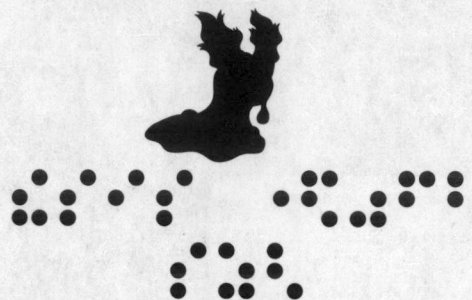

SIGH
...

GLARE

...ARE
YOU?!

WHO
...

SUBMARINE EXPLORER'S AUTO-DIVE FUNCTION HAS KICKED IN!

DID RUBY DO THAT TO LURE THAT THUG AWAY FROM US?!

ALTHOUGH I DON'T UNDER-STAND WHY YOU WERE **HIDING** YOUR SKILLS INSTEAD OF USING THEM!

WHAT-EVER...

AHA! YOU'RE QUITE A SKILLED TRAINER, AREN'T YOU? I CAN TELL!

LET'S SEE IF YOUR SKILLS CAN HANDLE THIS!!

WHEN SHE'S REALLY DOWN AND OUT, SHE LIGHTS HER MATCHES...AND SEES VISIONS IN THE FLAME...

IT'S ABOUT A POOR LITTLE GIRL WHO SELLS MATCHES TO SURVIVE.

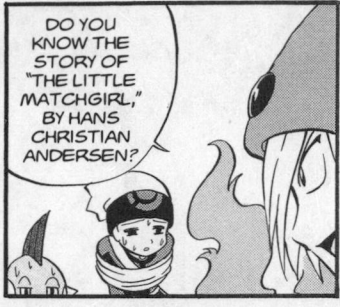

DO YOU KNOW THE STORY OF "THE LITTLE MATCHGIRL," BY HANS CHRISTIAN ANDERSEN?

...THINGS THAT AREN'T REALLY THERE !!

KRKL KR KL

AND THE HEAT WILL MAKE YOU SEE THINGS ...

IT'S AS HOT AS IT CAN GET IN HERE...

W'FF

MY FIRES ARE LIKE THAT.

FOOSH

GOGM !!

SWSH

SHATTR

AHHH!!!

ILLUSIONS CREATED OUT OF A FLICKERING FLAME...

SHVVR SHVVR

IT'S REALLY SOMETHING, ISN'T IT?

BLAISE THE...

...ILLUSIONIST...

HA HA HA! THAT IS WHY EVERYBODY CALLS ME...

I'M SORRY I GOT YOU INVOLVED IN ALL THIS...

IT'S NOT YOUR FAULT... I'M JUST WORRIED ABOUT RUBY.

WHY DO THEY WANT SUBMARINE EXPLORER 1?!

WHAT ARE THOSE MEN AFTER, ANYWAY?!

IT'S NO USE. IT'S BROKEN.

THUNK

CAN'T YOU RECALL THAT SUBMARINE?!

SINCE THEY NEED THAT COMPONENT TO MAKE IT WORK PROPERLY...ALL YOU NEED TO DO IS CANCEL THE MANUFACTURING OF THAT PART!!

YOU SAID THE SUBMARINE WON'T BE COMPLETE WITHOUT THAT CORE COMPONENT THINGIE...

HMM! I'VE GOT IT!! I'VE JUST THOUGHT OF A PLAN!!

SMAK

UM...

WELL? WHAT DO YOU THINK...?

THEN, NO MATTER WHAT THEY'RE AFTER, THEY'LL NEVER BE ABLE TO GET IT!!

HUH?

THE DEVON CORPORATION'S PRESIDENT STONE WAS GOING TO PERSONALLY DELIVER IT THE OTHER DAY, BUT...

WHAT?!

ACTUALLY... THE COMPONENT IS ALREADY MADE.

THIS COMPONENT IS SOMETHING PRESIDENT STONE DEVELOPED ON HIS OWN— IN SECRECY. NO ONE ELSE AT THE COMPANY EVEN KNOWS OF ITS EXISTENCE.

...ACCORDING TO THE NEWS, HE WAS ATTACKED BY A WILD POKÉMON WHILE TAKING HIS DAILY STROLL. HE'S STILL UNCONSCIOUS AT A HOSPITAL.

AHHHHH...

TO TELL THE TRUTH...WE HAVE NO IDEA WHERE IT IS RIGHT NOW.

DAD!!

SMASH

DAD!!
SHATTR

DAD...
DAD!!
DAD!! SHATTR   SHATTR

DAD!!!

DAD, I LOVE IT WHEN YOU TEACH ME HOW TO POKÉMON BATTLE!

DAD! I WANNA GET STRONGER!

TROMBL

HEH...

...WHATEVER IT WAS, IT MUST BE HIS WORST NIGHTMARE.

THE ILLUSIONS GOT THE BEST OF HIM. I DON'T KNOW WHAT HE SAW INSIDE THE FIRE, BUT...

FWUMP

I'M SURE THIS ATTACK IS VERY EFFECTIVE AGAINST OTHER PEOPLE.

...A MIS-TAKE...

THAT WAS...

AND I DID SEE MY WORST NIGHTMARE... LIKE YOU SAID...

!!

...IS ALSO MY **BEST** MEMORY— AND IT'S WHAT KEEPS ME GOING!!!

BUT MY WORST NIGHT-MARE...

TING

MUMU!!

BY THE WAY...YOU ASKED ME HOW I WAS ABLE TO TELL THAT YOUR SLUGMA WAS QUIET NATURED...

RMBL

FSST

AN EMERGENCY EXIT...?!

COME BACK, MUMU!!

SWOOP

FOOM

WHAT?!

MY QUESTION TO YOU IS, WHY CAN'T **YOU** TELL THINGS LIKE THAT?

FSSMAK

I CAN SENSE THE NATURE OF A POKÉMON FROM ITS MOVES AND BODY LANGUAGE— EVEN IF WE'VE JUST MET.

IF YOU PAY CAREFUL ATTENTION TO THEM, I'M SURE YOU COULD TOO.

WZZZ

20

...BY MY FATHER.

AT LEAST, THAT'S WHAT I WAS TAUGHT...

IT'S MISSING SOME SORT OF SPECIAL CORE COMPONENT MADE BY THE DEVON CORPORATION!

OH...! AND I'VE FOUND OUT WHAT THE PROBLEM IS!!

I GOT SUBMARINE EXPLORER 1!

BOSS...

AS SOON AS WE INSTALL THAT...

...WE'LL BE ABLE TO GET TO THE LOWEST DEPTHS OF THE HOENN SEA AND...

...THE SEA-FLOOR CAVERN!!

ADVENTURE MAP

SAPPHIRE

RUBY

CHIC
Combusken ♀
Lv19

RONO
Lairon ♂
Lv34

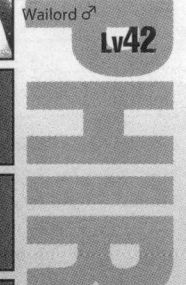

LORRY
Wailord ♂
Lv42

Route 109

Slateport City | Slateport City

Route 110

MUMU
Marshtomp ♂

NANA
Mightyena ♀

KIKI
Delcatty ♀

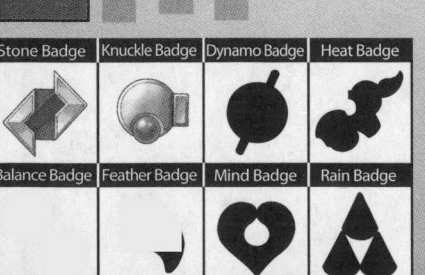

Stone Badge	Knuckle Badge	Dynamo Badge	Heat Badge
Balance Badge	Feather Badge	Mind Badge	Rain Badge

		Cool	Beauty	Cute	Smart	Tough
Super	Normal					
Master	Hyper					

● Chapter 203 ●
I'm Your Biggest Fan, Donphan

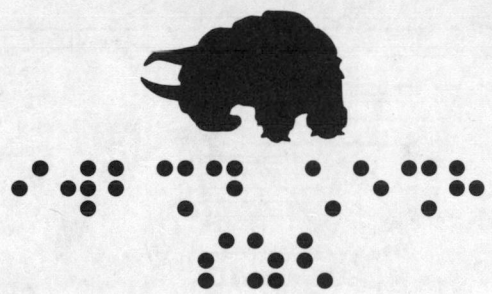

ROUTE 110

THIS STEVEN GUY HAS SPLIT FROM DEWFORD TOWN ALREADY... I'M GONNA HAVE TO FIND HIM.

SIGH. WHAT SHOULD I DO...?

DEVON CORPORA

BUT COME TO THINK OF IT...

ROUTE 110

SLATEPORT CITY

...I DON'T HAVE A CLUE WHERE HE WENT!

28

WE WERE ONLY TRYING TO CAPTURE THAT DONPHAN OVER THERE.

AH... I'M SORRY. TERRIBLY SORRY.

HE'S FAMOUS AROUND HERE. PEOPLE CALL HIM THE "TRICK MASTER."

AND THIS IS TRICKY.

I'M WATT-SON.

NO. THE ONLY WHATZIT... ER...GADGET I MADE WAS THE ONE TO CATCH THAT DONPHAN.

WHAT'RE YA SO EXCITED ABOUT? ISN'T THAT YER WHATZIT?

THE GROUND FLIPPED OVER?!

I GET ATTACKED BY WHATZITS AND BEFORE THAT THE GROUND FLIPS OVER AND I ALMOST FALL INTO AN UNDER-GROUND CAVE OR SOMETHIN'!!

I DON'T GET THIS TOWN AT ALL...

!!

I THINK SO, TRICKY !!

COULD THIS BE IT, WATTY ?!

● Chapter 204 ●
Plugging Past Electrike I

The Fourth Chapter

UMM... SOMEWHERE 'ROUND HERE...

SNFF SNFF

SNFF

YAY! THERE IT IS!

COME ON, LITTLE GIRL. TELL US. WHERE IS IT?

WELCOME TO MAUVILLE CITY

WHERE IS IT?

OKAY!

SWISH SWISH

HURRY UP AND OPEN IT!

WE'VE BEEN LOOKING FOR THIS ENTRANCE FOR YEARS!!

THAT'S RIGHT!

HERE? SO THIS IS SOME KIND OF... DOOR?

SPIN

OOH!!

YEAH!!

AH! HERE YOU ARE!! OKAY... COME AND GET IT!!

WE CHAL-LENGE YOU!!

WATT-SON!!

FWIP FWIP

BUT... WHAT'S THE STORY BEHIND THIS UNDER-GROUND CITY ANY-WAY?

WELL, IT'S...

BOM

BOM

HUH ?!

NO WONDER. HE'S A GYM LEADER. HE CAN'T BE BEATEN **THAT** EASY.

YOU'RE TOO STRONG, WATT-SON.

OOOH.

THAT'S RIGHT! IF YOU WANT TO BEAT A GYM LEADER, YOU'RE GOING TO HAVE TO GET A **LEAD** ON ME!! HAR HAR HAR!!

YOU'RE A GYM LEADER ?!

WHAT...? I'M GIVING THEM GYM BADGES AS PROOF OF THEIR PAR-TICIPATION IN A GYM BATTLE.

GRAB

WHAT D'YOU THINK YOU'RE DOIN'?!!

HEY !!

BUT YOUR ATTACKS WERE PRETTY GOOD. HERE YOU GO. HERE ARE YOUR DYNAMO BADGES.

HURRAY!

...GYM BATTLE?! YOU CALL **THAT** A GYM BATTLE ?!

YAY! HURRAY !!

ANYONE MAY CHALLENGE ME WHENEVER THEY WANT TO— AND THAT COUNTS AS THEIR GYM BATTLE!!

THAT'S RIGHT! I'M THE GYM LEADER OF MAUVILLE CITY. MY MOTTO? "CHALLENGE ME ANYTIME, ANYWHERE!"

THOSE KIDS HAD PIZZAZZ. I DON'T SEE ANYTHING WRONG WITH GIVING THEM BADGES.

BY THE AUTHORITY VESTED IN ME BY THE POKÉMON ASSOCIATION, I MAY GIVE OUT BADGES AS I SEE FIT.

BUT... WHAT ABOUT WINNING AND LOSING?

ARE YOU KID-DING ?!

THAT'S A JOKE, BY THE WAY. HAR HAR...

ER...

IF YOU HAVE THE GUMPTION TO **BADGER** ME... I'LL BE HAPPY TO **BADGE** YOU.

TADA

DO YOU COLLECT BADGES TOO...?

THAT'S GREAT! HERE! YOU JUST EARNED YOUR DYNAMO BADGE FOR FINDING THE ENTRANCE TO THE UNDERGROUND CITY FOR US.

ZI P

OOH ...

SL AP

RMBLRMBLRM...!!

IT'S COMING RIGHT AT US!!

AAAAAAH!

SPIN

SLAM

KA-DUNK

HEY...

OW.

OW.

ARE YOU ALL RIGHT?! HANG IN THERE!!

SLAP SLAP SLA

YOU WANT A PIECE OF ME?!

TAKE THIS... AND THIS!!

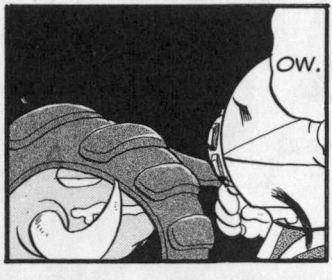

OW.

SMASH

STOP IT, WILL YA?!!

LIGHTS ON!!

KLTTR
KLTTR

I'VE FINALLY MADE IT TO THE UNDER-GROUND CITY OF NEW MAUVILLE!!

AH... YES. OF COURSE.

PULL

...WAS SAID TO BE CONSTRUCTED BY OUR ANCESTORS. BUT WE WERE NEVER ABLE TO PROVE ITS EXISTENCE—UNTIL **NOW**.

VERY WELL... AS I TOLD YOU, THE CITY OF NEW MAUVILLE...

WHAT DID YOU SEE BEFORE WE FELL DOWN HERE?

AND WHAT'S THAT?

NOBODY KNOWS WHY THE CITY WAS BUILT. BUT WE HAVE A HYPOTHESIS...

OUR ANCES-TORS...

...MIGHT HAVE HAD THE SAME PROBLEM— AND THIS SEEMS TO HAVE BEEN THEIR SOLUTION!

...BUT SINCE THE CITY IS SO SMALL, WE'VE ALWAYS HAD A SHORTAGE OF PLAY-GROUNDS AND WHATNOT.

MAUVILLE CITY HAS A GREAT NUMBER OF YOUNG PEOPLE...

CHILDREN, RIGHT...? LOTS AND LOTS OF CHILDREN.

THIS IS EXACTLY WHAT WE WERE HOPING TO DISCOVER.

BOTH WATTY AND I LOVE CHILDREN.

AND **THAT** CAN SUB-STITUTE FOR MY GYM BATTLE !!

I'LL HELP YA!! HOWEVER I CAN!!

I GET IT! SO YOU TWO WANNA INVESTIGATE THE SECRET BEHIND THIS UNDERGROUND CITY, RIGHT?! IN THAT CASE...

IN THAT CASE ...?

Hear me...

hear me...

hear me...

I CAN'T ACCEPT THE BADGE WITHOUT DOIN' **SOMETHIN'**!!

IS THAT OKAY WITH YOU, MISTER WATTSON?! ANSWER ME IF YOU CAN HEAR ME!!

SURE! SOUNDS GREAT! NOW COULD YOU COME DOWN HERE? RIGHT AWAY...?!

AH! IT'S WATTY'S ELECTRIKE AND MAGNEMITE!!

FWIP FWIP

HE'S OVER THERE!!

B-T-P

WHAT'S THE MAT-TER?!

WHAT THE...?

FWLUMP

HMM...

MAGNEMITE CAN'T FLY IF THEIR INTERNAL ELECTRICAL SUPPLY IS DEPLETED!

AREA　NO.082 Magnemite
Magnet Pokémon
Height: 1' 00"
Height: 13.2 lbs

Magnemite attaches itself to power lines to feed on electricity. Check your house has a power outage, check your circuit breaker. You may find a large number of this Pokémon clinging to the breaker box.

AND IT'S STILL HAPPENING!!

THAT'S RIGHT!

SO YOU MEAN THESE MAGNEMITE HAD THEIR ELECTRICITY "SUCKED OUT" BY SOMETHING... OR SOMEBODY?!

TAKE ME TO HIM, ELECTRIKE!!

WHERE ARE YOU, WATTY?!

● Chapter 205 ●
Plugging Past Electrike II

SMASH

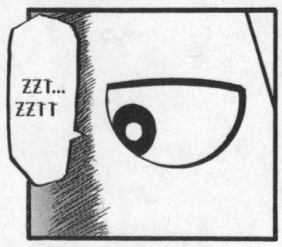

ZZT... ZZTT

AND IT'S USING THE ELECTRICITY IT GENERATES TO ATTACK US!!

FWSSSH

IT'S A HUGE GENER- ATOR!!

PRETTY SNEAKY...

OH MY... IT'S NOT **JUST** A GENERATOR THEN?!

ZZZZZT!! zz

PLLOOP

TURN POP

FWSSH

WELL, TWO CAN PLAY THAT GAME, YOU KNOW !!

WHAT'RE YOU DOIN' ?!

TINK TINK

KTINK

FWISSSH

ZZZ ZZT

ZZZZZZ

AIYEEE!!

KRASH

WHAT THE—?!

THAT'S WHAT I WAS SAYIN' !!

I DON'T THINK I CAN BEAT IT!!

HUH ?

SO WHAT DO WE DO NOW?

IT FEELS LIKE...I'VE GOT... MOTION SICKNESS OR SOME- THING!!

WHAT'S GOIN' ON?! I CAN'T RUN STRAIGHT !!

KRASH

THUD

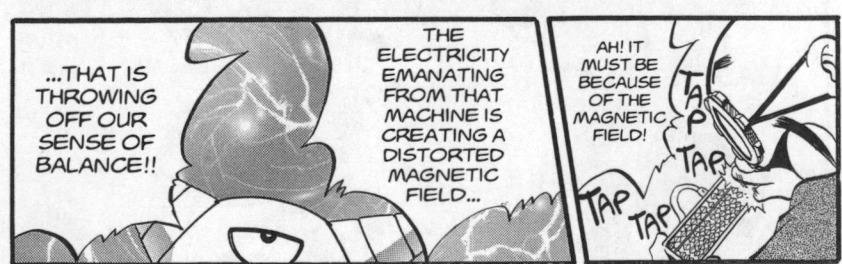

...THAT IS THROWING OFF OUR SENSE OF BALANCE!!

THE ELECTRICITY EMANATING FROM THAT MACHINE IS CREATING A DISTORTED MAGNETIC FIELD...

AH! IT MUST BE BECAUSE OF THE MAGNETIC FIELD!

TAP TAP TAP TAP

YOU WANTED TO **WARN** US. THAT'S WHY YOU WERE CAUSIN' ALL THAT TROUBLE !!

I GET IT!! YOU SENSED THE CHANGE IN THE MAGNETIC FIELD, DIDN'TCHA?!

OH...

WHAT'S THE MATTER?

SNORT

I BET IT SENSED THE CHANGE IN THE ELECTRO-MAGNETIC FIELD!!

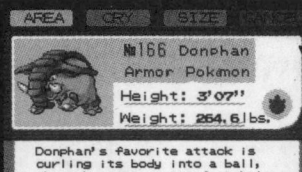

AREA　CRY　SIZE　DATA

№166 Donphan
Armor Pokémon
Height: 3'07''
Weight: 264.6 lbs.

Donphan's favorite attack is curling its body into a ball, then charging at its foe while rolling at high speed. Once it starts rolling, this Pokémon can't stop very easily.

DONPHAN IS A POKÉMON WHO CURLS ITS BODY UP AND ROLLS TO MOVE...

COME TO THINK OF IT... THE SPOT THIS DONPHAN WAS RUNNING AROUND WAS RIGHT ABOVE THIS GENERATOR!!

THE ELECTRIC ATTACKS ARE TERRIFYING ENOUGH AS IT IS—BUT WE CAN'T EVEN STAND UPRIGHT!

KERASH

SMASH

SMAK

BUT WE'RE IN EVEN BIGGER TROUBLE NOW!!

WE HAVE TO SAVE MR. WATTSON AT LEAST!!

DON'T GIVE UP!!!

THAT'S RIGHT!

WE'LL SAVE YOU, WATTY!!

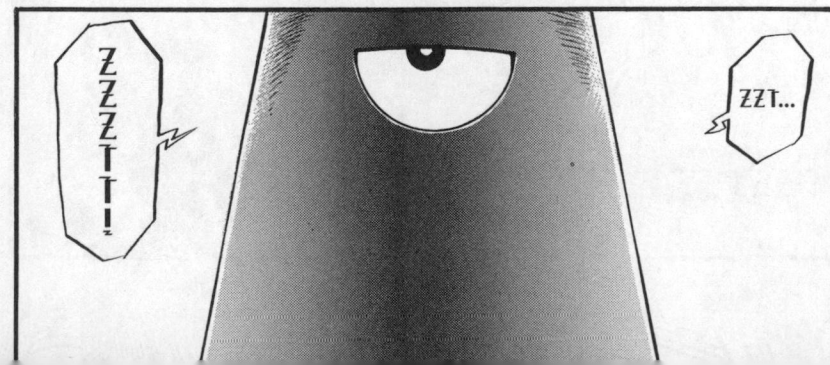

ZZZZT!!

ZZT...

TAP TAP

I'LL FIG-URE OUT...

...A WAY TO STOP THAT ROGUE GENER-ATOR!!

DON'T YOU WORRY! I HAVE TONS OF TRICKS UP MY SLEEVE!!

I'M SORRY, TRICKY...

PANT!

PANT!

AHA!! I'VE GOT IT!!

TAP

ABSORB AND DIS-CHARGE...!!

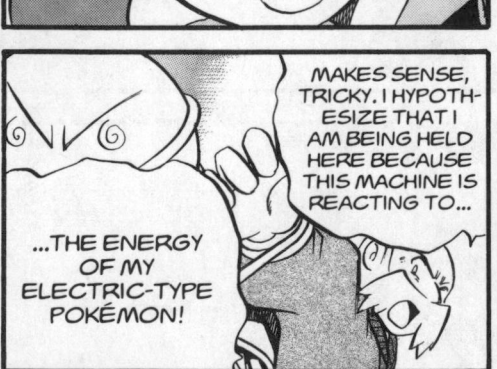

MAKES SENSE, TRICKY. I HYPOTH-ESIZE THAT I AM BEING HELD HERE BECAUSE THIS MACHINE IS REACTING TO...

...THE ENERGY OF MY ELECTRIC-TYPE POKÉMON!

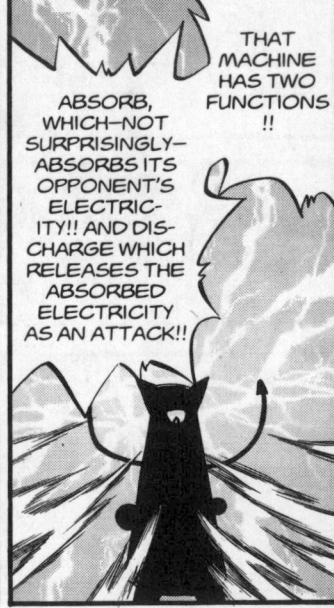

THAT MACHINE HAS TWO FUNCTIONS!!

ABSORB, WHICH—NOT SURPRISINGLY—ABSORBS ITS OPPONENT'S ELECTRIC-ITY!! AND DIS-CHARGE WHICH RELEASES THE ABSORBED ELECTRICITY AS AN ATTACK!!

THEN ...

IF IT'S REPEATIN' ITS MOVES LIKE ABSORB → DISCHARGE → ABSORB → DISCHARGE...THAT MEANS IT'S GONNA ABSORB AFTER IT DISCHARGES, RIGHT?!

OKAY THEN!

...THAT'S OUR CHANCE TO **RUSH** IT!!

...WHEN IT STARTS TO ABSORB AGAIN...

ZWOOP

COURSE IT IS!!

I UNDER-STAND WHAT YOU MEAN, BUT...ARE YOU SURE THAT'S POS-SIBLE?!

GO! GO! GO!!

FOOM

MISTER GYM LEADER! I'M GONNA BORROW YOUR ELECTRIKE FOR A SEC, OKAY...?

NOW!!

ZZZT

BUUM

BZZZT

THUD

FWUOOMP

YOUR GROUND-TYPE POKÉMON HAVE A GOOD ADVANTAGE OVER ELECTRIC-TYPES!!

SMAK

I'M REAL GLAD YOU WERE HERE!!

ZOOP

I want to play!!

WHOA!

KICK

HMPH. WHAT KIND OF MADMAN WOULD CREATE SUCH AN ANNOYING MACHINE?!

PING

WHAT?

THERE'S SOMETHING INSCRIBED HERE...

HUH?

My Dear Unknown Descendants of the Future, This gadget is my invention! If you ever find this place (which, if you're reading this, you must have), feel free to push the red button and play to your heart's content! Har har har!!!

...MISTER... TRICK?!

SINCERELY, MISTER TRICK, GENIUS.

KRCKL

KRCKL

KRCKL

PUSH

OOH!

KLANG

YOUR ANCESTOR, DEAR TRICKY!

YOU MEAN... THE MAN WHO BUILT THIS GENERATOR, NOT TO MENTION NEW MAUVILLE... IS...

TNKTNKTNK

RMBLRMB

OHHH!! THE ENTIRE CITY HAS TURNED INTO AN ENORMOUS PLAYGROUND!!

TRICKY!!

WATTY!!

MY ANCESTOR WAS A REMARKABLE MAN, WASN'T HE?!!

YES. NEW MAUVILLE REALLY WAS A HUGE AMUSEMENT PARK FOR CHILDREN— JUST AS WE THOUGHT!

YOU WERE RIGHT AFTER ALL.

A FEW DAYS LATER...

UH-HUH! AND I **ANCEST** THAT YOU SHOW YOUR GRATITUDE TO HIM! HAR HAR HAR!!

ADVENTURE MAP

SAPPHIRE

  CHIC
Combusken♀
Lv21

 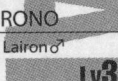 RONO
Lairon♂
Lv34

 LORRY
Wailord♂
Lv42

 PHADO
Donphan♂
Lv39

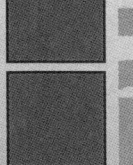

RUBY

 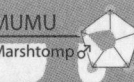 MUMU
Marshtomp♂

 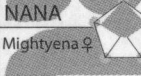 NANA
Mightyena♀

 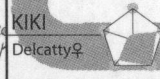 KIKI
Delcatty♀

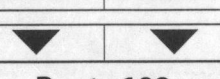

Route 109

| Slateport City | Slateport City |

Route 110

Mauville City

New Mauville

Badges

Stone Badge	Knuckle Badge	Dynamo Badge	Heat Badge

Balance Badge	Feather Badge	Mind Badge	Rain Badge
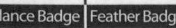			

Contest Ribbons

	Cool	Beauty	Cute	Smart	Tough
Normal	🟊	🟊	🟊	🟊	🟊
Super	🟊	🟊	🟊	🟊	🟊
Hyper			🟊	🟊	🟊
Master	🟊		🟊	🟊	🟊

● Chapter 206 ●
Not So Fetching Feebas

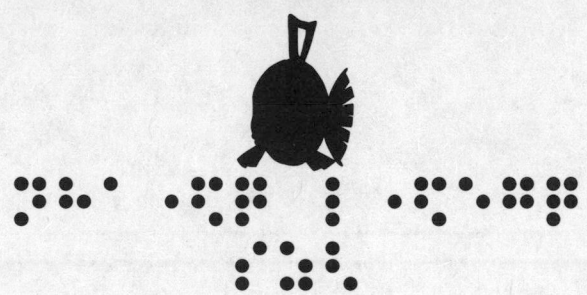

The Fourth Chapter

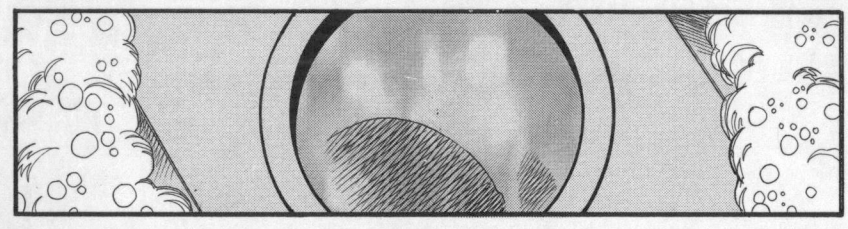

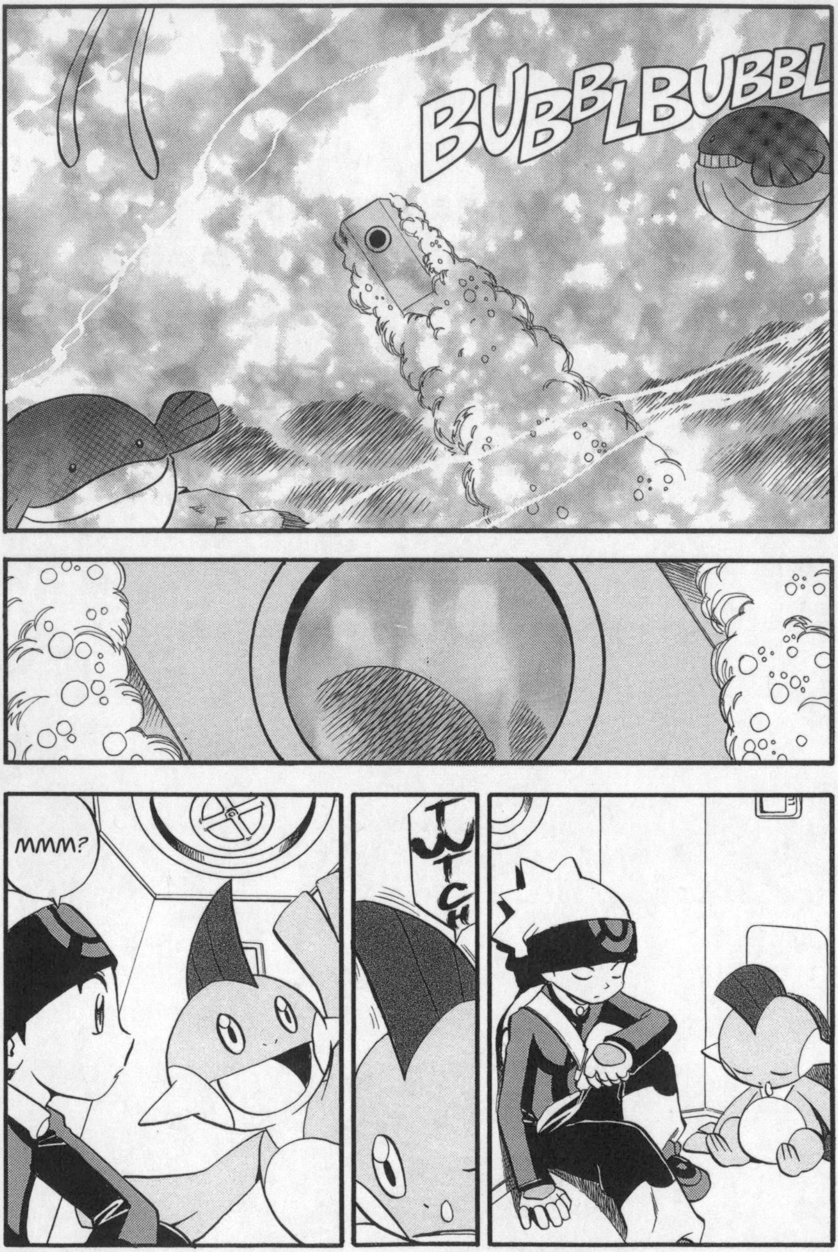

MMM?

SPLASH

BUBBLBUBBL

PFFFT

PHEW. I WONDER HOW FAR WE'VE TRAVELED...

KLICK

...ROUTE 118?!

THE SUB-MARINE GOT THIS FAR...

...WHILE I WAS FIGHTING THAT GUY INSIDE ?!!

WAIT... THIS IS...

BREAK-ING NEWS!

I HOPE THE PRESIDENT, CAPTAIN STERN, AND MR. DOCK ARE ALL RIGHT...

SUBMARINE EXPLORER 1 STOLEN!!

No Entry

AN UNKNOWN PERSON OR PERSONS HAVE BROKEN INTO THE SHIPYARD AT SLATEPORT CITY!!

WE'RE LIVE ON THE SCENE TO REPORT ON THE THEFT OF SUBMARINE EXPLORER 1!!

CAPTAIN STERN, THE SUPERVISOR MR. DOCK, AND SOME CIVILIANS WERE INVOLVED AS WELL. WE'VE ALSO LEARNED THAT ONE OF THE CIVILIANS IS A YOUNG BOY... BUT DETAILS ARE UNCLEAR!!

ACCORDING TO CAPTAIN STERN, A GROUP OF THUGS WEARING RED UNIFORMS ATTACKED THIS SHIPYARD!!

SO... WHAT DO I DO NOW?

BUT I GUESS IT IS A BIG DEAL. THAT STOLEN SUBMARINE WAS ABOUT TO BE USED FOR THE UNDERSEA EXPLORATION OF THE HOENN REGION...

YIKES! THEY'RE MAKING A PRETTY BIG DEAL OUT OF IT!

AND DAD WILL FIND OUT WHERE I AM!!

Boy From Submarine Robbery Found!!

IF I CONTINUE ON MY JOURNEY, THE PRESIDENT AND THE OTHERS WON'T KNOW THAT I'M SAFE. SHOULD I GO BACK TO SLATEPORT...?

THEN I'LL BE ON THE NEWS AGAIN...

NO!! I CAN'T DO THAT!!

DRIP

I PROMISE I'LL COME BACK TO SEE YOU ONCE I FULFILL MY DREAM... MY DREAM OF BECOMING THE CHAMPION OF POKÉMON CONTESTS!!

YOU WERE THE FIRST PERSON WHO REALLY UNDERSTOOD ME IN HOENN!!

I'M SORRY, MR. PRESIDENT...

WHEN ARE WE GOING TO LIVE TOGETHER AGAIN AS A FAMILY?!

NORMAN WENT LOOKING FOR YOU...AND HE HASN'T COME BACK EITHER...

WHEN, OH WHEN, ARE YOU GOING TO COME HOME...?

RUBY...

SHORTLY THEREAFTER, THEY BOTH DISAPPEARED INTO THE DEPTHS OF THE SEA!

HE ENTERED THE SUBMARINE WITH THE MYSTERIOUS INTRUDER.

WE HAVE EXCLUSIVE SURVEILLANCE FOOTAGE OF THE BOY INVOLVED IN THE ROBBERY!!

RUBY!!

OHHH...

THIS ESCAPE POD IS PRETTY HANDY!

HEH...

WHOAA!!

I'LL RIDE IT UNTIL I GET CLOSE TO A TOWN OR SOMETHING!

WHAT?!

AAAAAH!!

UH... SORRY!

WELL? WHAT ARE YOU GONNA DO ABOUT IT?!

HUH?

DUDE!! YOU TOTALLY RUINED MY FISHING TACKLE!!

YOU'RE GONNA STAY HERE AND HELP ME FISH!!

SORRY WON'T CUT IT!!

WHAT?! BUT I'M IN A HURRY!

NGH...

SERIOUSLY? YOU'RE GONNA JUST WALK AWAY AFTER THE MESS YOU'VE MADE?!

UH... SO WHAT DO YOU WANT ME TO DO?

GOOD! THAT'S MORE LIKE IT!

I'LL HELP HIM OUT FOR A LITTLE WHILE... THEN I'LL TALK MY WAY OUT OF THIS.

GREAT. NOW I'VE GOTTEN MYSELF MIXED UP WITH **THIS** WEIRDO ...

I'M SURE YOU WON'T BE CATCHING THE POKÉMON I'M AFTER ANYTIME SOON, BUT TWO LINES ARE BETTER THAN ONE.

ALL YOU HAFTA DO IS DROP THE LINE IN THE WATER.

HERE! TAKE THIS FISHING ROD...

AGH!! WHAT IS THIS THING ?!

OH!

POINK POINK

YEAH!

SPLOOSH

HEY... LOOK, I'M SORRY I SHOUTED AT YOU...

THIS CAN'T BE THE POKÉMON HE'S AFTER.

I'VE NEVER SEEN THIS POKÉMON BEFORE, AND...IT'S UNBELIEVABLY UGLY!!

BYE-BYE.

SPLASH

THIS ONE AGAIN ?!

I'VE BEEN HERE FOR TEN DAYS STRAIGHT WITHOUT ANY LUCK. YOU CAN IMAGINE HOW FRUSTRATED I AM.

KERSPLASH

EWW! AGAIN ?!

IF I COULD ONLY GET MY HANDS ON THIS POKÉMON...

KA-SPLOOSH

WILL YOU CUT IT OUT?!

Did it! ♬

THE IMPORTANT THING IN FISHING IS KNOWING WHERE TO SINK YOUR LINE. ONCE YOU FIND THE RIGHT SPOT, IT'S A PIECE OF CAKE.

HUH ?

HUH ?

IT'S CALLED A FEEBAS AND IT LOOKS LIKE THIS.

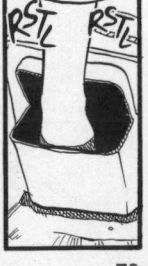

IT'S NOT EXACTLY THE BEST-LOOKING POKÉMON... BUT IT IS REALLY RARE. LOOK HERE...

RSTL RSTL

70

GLOOM

UM
...

I ALMOST HAD A FEEBAS ...

IT'S NO USE... YOU HAVE NO IDEA WHERE YOU CAUGHT IT, DO YOU?

WHAT ?

UM ...

DON'T WORRY. IT'S NOT YOUR FAULT.

OH WELL! I'LL JUST HAVE TO GET OVER THIS SETBACK AND START OVER!

I NEVER IMAGINED ANYONE WOULD WANT AN UGLY POKÉMON LIKE THAT...

I PREFER POKÉMON WHO ARE CUTE AND BEAUTIFUL MYSELF... ONES THAT I CAN ENTER IN POKÉMON CONTESTS.

AHA HA HA!

YOU AND YOUR POKÉMON ARE SO WELL GROOMED!

WELL, THAT MAKES SENSE ...

HA HA... IN CONTESTS, HUH?

IT'S JUST THAT I HEARD IT WAS SUPER RARE AND A LOT OF OTHER PEOPLE WANT TO GET THEIR HANDS ON IT. I FIGURED I COULD MAKE SOME MONEY WITH IT...

BUT I'M NOT AFTER IT BECAUSE I HAVE A THING FOR UGLY POKÉMON.

LIKE YOU SAY, THE FEEBAS ISN'T EXACTLY THE BEST-LOOKING POKÉMON AROUND.

HA HA HA! I GUESS THAT'S WHAT I GET FOR BEING GREEDY!

...I'D BE PRETTY DEPRESSED TOO!

SO...

I BET IF I WERE JUST ABOUT TO GET AHOLD OF THIS POKÉMON... AND FAILED TO CAPTURE IT IN THE LAST MINUTE...

I'VE BEEN LOOKING FOR A CERTAIN POKÉMON TOO...

I KNOW I'LL BE ECSTATICALLY HAPPY WHEN I FINALLY MEET THIS POKÉMON!

I'D FEEL BAD LETTING IT END LIKE THIS. I'LL HELP YOU!

I'M GABBY, FROM HOENN TV.

THERE'S SOMETHING I'D LIKE TO DISCUSS WITH YOU... IN PRIVATE !!

SLATEPORT SHIPYARD

CAPTAIN STERN!

WHO ARE YOU?

HEY, WAIT!

YANK

COULD YOU SPARE A MOMENT OF YOUR TIME?!

ACCORDING TO NEWS REPORTS, PRESIDENT STONE WAS ATTACKED BY A WILD POKÉMON WHILE TAKING A WALK.

I KNOW EVEN MORE! PRESIDENT STONE WAS IN AN ACCIDENT. YOU HAVE NO IDEA OF THE WHEREABOUTS OF THAT COMPONENT, DO YOU?

THAT IS... CORRECT.

HOW DO YOU KNOW ABOUT THAT?!

AM I RIGHT ?

YOU WERE WAITING FOR THE DEVON CORPORATION'S PRESIDENT STONE TO BRING A SPECIAL COMPONENT HERE...

I APOLOGIZE FOR BEING SO FORWARD, BUT...

● Chapter 207 ●
On the Loose and Hyper with Zangoose and Seviper I

REMEMBER ME? GABBY FROM HOENN TV. I INTERVIEWED YOU THE OTHER DAY!

YOU'RE NORMAN, THE NEW GYM LEADER OF PETALBURG CITY, AREN'T YOU?!

HAVING A SKILLED GYM LEADER ON OUR SIDE IS EVEN BETTER THAN WORKING WITH THE POLICE!!

HE'S INVESTIGATING THIS CASE... I BET HE'LL HELP US!! ISN'T THIS FORTUITOUS?!

THAT ISN'T WHAT I WANT TO KNOW!!

THE DEVON CORPORATION'S PRESIDENT STONE WAS ATTACKED AND THE SPECIAL SUBMARINE COMPONENT HE WAS TRANSPORTING WAS STOLEN NEAR PETALBURG WOODS!

WE'LL TELL YOU EVERYTHING WE KNOW!

OH!

PUSH

HE HAD HIS CASTFORM WITH HIM. WE'RE TAKING CARE OF IT FOR THE TIME BEING AND—

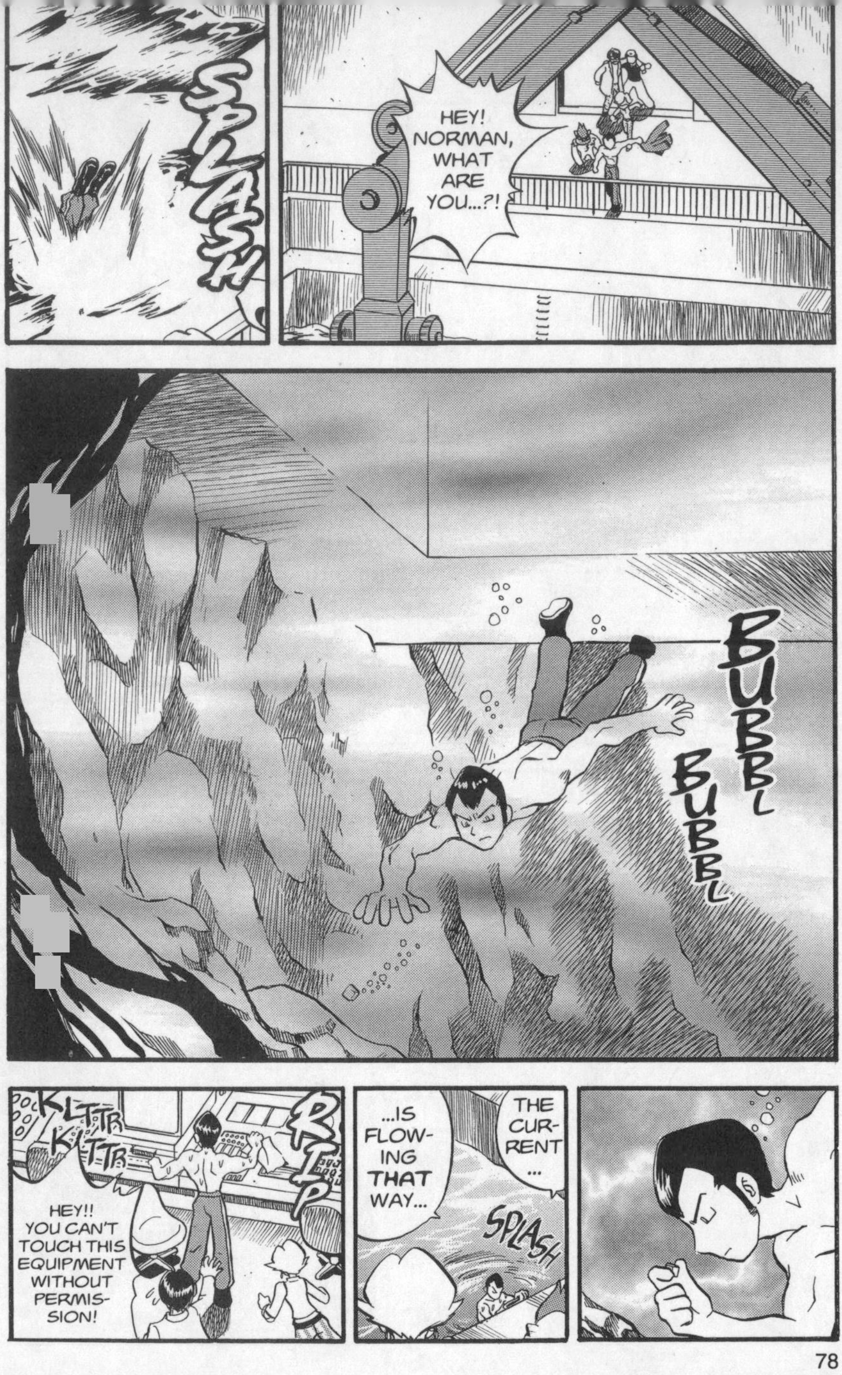

HEY! NORMAN, WHAT ARE YOU...?!

SPLASH

BUBBL BUBBL BUBBL

KLT-TR KLT-TR

RIP

HEY!! YOU CAN'T TOUCH THIS EQUIPMENT WITHOUT PERMISSION!

...IS FLOWING THAT WAY...

THE CURRENT...

SPLASH

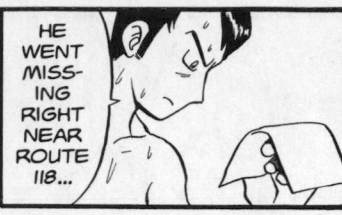

HE WENT MISSING RIGHT NEAR ROUTE 118...

I'M LOOKING FOR MY SON! HE RAN AWAY RIGHT AFTER WE MOVED HERE!!

I WANT TO TRACK HIM DOWN— AND THAT'S ALL!!

IT HAS THE SURVEILLANCE FOOTAGE AND NAVIGATIONAL DATA FROM SUBMARINE EXPLORER 1.

I'M TAKING THIS WITH ME.

WHAT ARE YOU DOING HERE THEN ...?!

SO THAT BOY IS YOUR...?!

KKK

VROOOM

NOR-MAN!!

PARDON THE INTRU-SION!

VRRR

YOU DON'T THINK SO? I DISAGREE.

HOW COME?

WELL, THAT WAS... STRANGE.

LET IT GO, GABBY!! WE'RE NOT GOING TO GET ANYTHING OUT OF HIM!!

AND IF WE TALK TO THAT BOY...

YOU SAW HOW DETERMINED HE WAS. I'M SURE HE'LL MANAGE TO FIND HIS SON!

TEAM AQUA IS RELATED TO THE INCIDENT WITH PRESIDENT STONE...

I DON'T THINK THIS IS THE SAME GROUP.

WHAT?! WHY?!

EXACTLY!

...HE'LL TELL US MORE ABOUT THIS MYSTERIOUS ORGANIZATION!

WE EVEN KNOW THEY'RE CALLED TEAM AQUA.

DO WE REALLY NEED TO TALK TO HIM THOUGH? WE ALREADY MET MEMBERS OF THE ORGANIZATION.

WHOA! YOU MEAN... THERE ARE **TWO** DIFFERENT ORGANI-ZATIONS BEHIND ALL THIS?!

BUT THE GROUP THAT ATTACKED THE SHIPYARD AND STOLE THE SUBMARINE WERE WEARING **RED** UNI-FORMS!!

THE GROUP WE SAW IN PETALBURG FOREST WERE WEARING **BLUE** UNIFORMS.

RSTL

HUH? WHAT'S THAT?

THERE'S SOMETHING IN THAT BUSH! GET DOWN!!

KRNCH

RSTL

YEAH...

SIGH... NO LUCK AT ALL. AND NIGHT HAS FALLEN.

IT'S A DUEL!!

№124 Seviper
Fang Snake Pokémon
Height: 8'10"
Weight: 115.7 lbs.

Seviper shares a generations-long feud with Zangoose. The scars on its body are evidence of vicious battles. This Pokémon attacks using its sword-edged tail.

№123 Zangoose
Cat Ferret Pokémon
Height: 4'03"
Weight: 88.8 lbs.

Memories of battling its arch-rival Seviper are etched into every cell of Zangoose's body. This Pokémon adroitly dodges attacks with incredible agility.

A ZANGOOSE AND A SEVIPER—TOGETHER!

WOW!!

IT'S NO USE!! WE INTERRUPTED THEIR SPECIAL BATTLE.

YOU DON'T WANT TO FIGHT US! YOU WANT TO FIGHT EACH OTHER! DON'T LET US GET IN YOUR WAY!!

AAAARGH!!

TOO LATE!!

TMP TMP TMP

WHAT?! MY POKÉNAV IS GONE!!

UM... MAP, MAP...

UH-OH... WHICH WAY SHOULD WE RUN?!

AAAH!

TINK TINK

NO WAY! YOU DO IT!

SCUFFLE SCUFFLE

HEY! USE YOUR POKÉMON TO LOSE THOSE TWO!!

SHINK

ADVENTURE MAP

SAPPHIRE

CHIC
Combusken ♀
Lv23

RONO
Lairon ♂
Lv35

LORRY
Wallord ♂
Lv42

PHADO
Donphan ♂
Lv40

RUBY

MUMU
Marshtomp ♂

NANA
Mightyena ♀

KIKI
Delcatty ♀

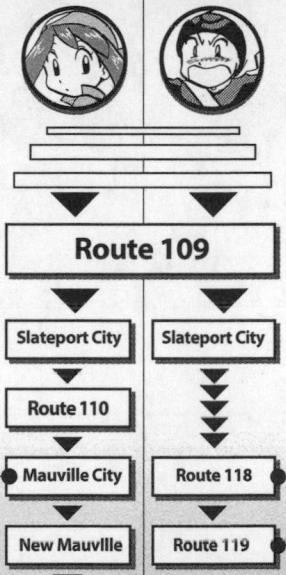

Route 109	**Route 109**
Slateport City	Slateport City
Route 110	
Mauville City	Route 118
New Mauvllle	Route 119
Route 111	

Stone Badge	Knuckle Badge	Dynamo Badge	Heat Badge
Balance Badge	Feather Badge	Mind Badge	Rain Badge

		Cool	Beauty	Cute	Smart	Tough
Super	Normal	👤	👤	👤	👤	👤
		👤	👤	👤	👤	👤
Master	Hyper	👤	👤	👤	👤	👤
		👤	👤	👤	👤	👤

● Chapter 208 ●
On the Loose and Hyper with Zangoose and Seviper II

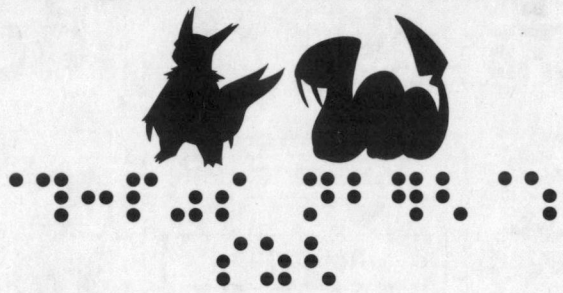

FWISH

PLUNGE

ACK!

SHATANG

PUSH PUSH

LIGHT SCREEN...?! IS THE FEEBAS DOING THAT?!

PHEW
...

MMM

OOO

94

THANKS TO YOUR... POKÉNAV?

WHAT'S WRONG?

DID YOU KNOW THERE WAS A BUILDING HERE?

I SURE DID— THANKS TO MY POKÉNAV.

THAT WAS CLOSE.

YOU OUGHT TO BE **THANKING** FEEBAS!!

Ick!! Why is it still hanging around!?

FEEBAS ...!!

IT MUST **LIKE** YOU!!

IT CAME TO DELIVER THE POKÉNAV YOU DROPPED INTO THE RIVER!!

THAT ISN'T SOMETHING YOU SEE EVERY DAY, YOU KNOW!!

LIGHT SCREEN TO BLOCK THE ATTACK! THEN MIRROR COAT TO DOUBLE THE DAMAGE AND REPEL IT BACK AT THEM!!

THINK ABOUT THE MOVES IT USED!!

AND IT'S NOT JUST THE POKÉNAV...

THE ONLY REASON WE'RE STILL STANDING IS BECAUSE OF THIS FEEBAS!!

ALL THAT TO HELP US!!

HUH?! NO WAY!!

TAKE THAT FEEBAS WITH YOU!!

ISN'T IT OBVIOUS?

YOU'RE RIGHT, BUT... WHAT EXACTLY SHOULD I DO ABOUT IT?

...I CAN'T LET MY GREED KEEP YOU TWO APART.

NAHHH. AFTER SEEING HOW FOND OF YOU THAT FEEBAS IS...

HMM...

BUT IT'S NOT A BEAUTIFUL POKÉMON! NOT ONE BIT... YEECH!

DON'T CONTRADICT ME!!

I KNOW... *YOU* TAKE IT!! YOU WANTED THIS POKÉMON TO BEGIN WITH. WELL, NOW IT'S ALL YOURS!!

BUT ONCE THIS KID GETS ATTACHED TO THE FEEBAS, I'LL CONVINCE HIM TO BREED THEM FOR ME, I'LL START A FEEBAS FARM!!

HEE HEE HEE! LOOKS LIKE THIS IS THE START OF A BEAUTIFUL RELATIONSHIP! WELL, MAYBE NOT **BEAUTIFUL**... I WOULDN'T MAKE MUCH SELLING ONE FEEBAS ANYWAY...

HMM...

HEH HEH HEH!

I'M A GENIUS!!

FLASH

GLOOM

ESPE-CIALLY BECAUSE OF **THESE** TWO!!

SMAK SMAK

MY TEAM IS GETTING FARTHER AND FARTHER AWAY FROM THE DREAM TEAM I IMAGINED!!

NO!!

WHERE ARE WE ANYWAY?

I'LL TAKE THE POKÉMON... FOR NOW. AND RELEASE IT LATER... SOMEWHERE.

FINE...

WELL? AS A POKÉMON TRAINER, HOW CAN YOU TURN YOUR BACK ON A POKÉMON WHO LIKES YOU SO MUCH?

"WEATHER... INSTITUTE"...?

P N K

P N K

P N K

IT'S BECAUSE IT'S NIGHTTIME. I'VE HEARD MACHINES RECORD THE METEOROLOGICAL DATA.

SO THIS IS WHERE WE ENDED UP AFTER RUNNING AWAY FROM ZANGOOSE AND SEVIPER... THE PLACE IS DESERTED!

PNK

!!

MNCH

PNK PNK

MNCH MNCH

OH! IT'S RAINING !!

? EH?

WHERE'S MUMU?

MUMU ?!!

HEY...

OH WELL. GUESS WE'LL JUST HAVE TO SHELTER HERE FOR THE NIGHT.

YOU DROPPED THEM WHEN YOU WERE RUNNING AROUND THE SHIPYARD AT SLATEPORT, REMEMBER? I PICKED THEM UP.

THEY **ARE** THE POKÉ-BLOCKS **YOU** MADE.

AND ALL BLENDED TO MATCH MUMU'S TASTE PREFERENCES. JUST LIKE THE POKÉBLOCKS I MADE...

TONS OF THEM ...

A POKÉ-BLOCK!

KRAKA-BOOM

BUT ONE THING I'M SURE OF IS THAT...

IT'S... KINDA HARD TO EXPLAIN AT THE MOMENT...

HEY!! WHAT'S GOING ON?!

SAVED BY THE THUNDER-CLAP!

...THE BIGGEST FAMILY SQUABBLE IN THE WORLD!

...YOU'RE ABOUT TO GET INVOLVED IN...

RMBLRMBLRMBL

● Chapter 209 ●
Hanging Around with Slaking I

VRMMVRMM

SIGH... WE DIDN'T LEARN ANYTHING SUBSTANTIAL AT THE SHIPYARD.

WOMWOMWOM

OH! THE CAST-FORM IS...

BUT WE CAN'T STOP PURSUING THIS STORY.

NOT AS LONG AS SOME EVIL ORGANIZA-TION IS LURKING IN THE SHAD-OWS OF THE HOENN REGION!

DRP

DRIP

IT'S RAIN-ING!

TO FIND THAT BOY WHO MET THE GANG IN THE RED UNIFORMS...BY FINDING THE BOY'S **FATHER**...WHO'S TRYING TO FIND **HIM**!!

FSSSS

ALL RIGHT! SO NOW WE'RE GOING... WHERE?

LET'S SEE WHAT WE CAN FIND OUT!

OUR TV STATION HAS GIVEN US THE GO-AHEAD TO FOLLOW UP ON THIS.

HOENN TELEVISION

SMAK

WHOA !!

SO LET'S STAKE OUT THE AREA...

HE SAID HE WAS GOING TO SEARCH AROUND ROUTE 118 AND ROUTE 119.

WE'VE BEEN TAKING CARE OF IT SINCE WE LEFT THE HOSPITAL... BUT IT JUST WON'T ACCEPT US!!

H-HEY, THAT'S DANGER-OUS!! WHAT'S IT DOING?! OUCH!!

SCREECH

THE WEATHER INSTI-TUTE ...?

WEATHER INSTITUTE

IS IT TRYING... TO GET OUTSIDE ?!

SMAK

SMAK

WAIT A MIN-UTE !!

!!

WHAT THE...? WHY?

KRAKABOOM

LOOK !!

WE HAVE TO INTERVIEW THAT BOY TO FIND OUT ABOUT THAT RED TEAM! LET'S GO, TY!!

AND NORMAN— THE GYM LEADER OF PET- ALBURG CITY!

I KNEW HE'D FIND HIS SON!!

SPLASH

THAT'S THE BOY, ISN'T IT?! THE ONE FROM THE SHIPYARD!!

I THINK SO!!

I'M GLAD YOU'RE OKAY, BUT YOU'RE IN BIG TROU-BLE!!

RUBY!

WHOA! THE FORCE OF THAT LIGHT-NING STRIKE KNOCKED YOU DOWN THE STAIRS! ARE YOU OKAY?

I'M FINE.

KRAKA BOON T-DNK T-DNK T-DN

THE BEST THING TO DO AT A TIME LIKE THIS IS APOLOGIZE AND GET IT OVER WITH!! MARK MY WORDS!

AND NOW HE'S TRYING TO DRAG YOU BACK HOME, HUH? WELL HERE'S SOME FRIENDLY ADVICE...

MY FATHER. I RAN AWAY FROM HOME. HE FOUND ME.

WHO IS THAT SCARY GUY?!

I COULD APOLOGIZE LIKE YOU SAY, OR... I COULD MAKE A RUN FOR IT... FIND A WAY OUT OF THIS PLACE... AND LOSE HIM IN THIS STORM.

I HAVE OPTIONS...

WHAT THE ...?!

KRI CK KRECK

HUH ?

KRIKK

BUT I HAVE A THIRD OPTION TOO...

KRECK

RIGHT HERE, RIGHT NOW!!!

HAVE A POKÉMON BATTLE WITH DAD!!

THEN HE'LL KNOW JUST HOW DETERMINED I AM!!!

I'LL FIGHT HIM AND WIN!!

...DON'T WATCH OUR BATTLE.

BLIP

ALSO, I HAVE A FAVOR TO ASK... PLEASE...

I KNOW APOLOGIZING TO HIM IS THE RIGHT THING TO DO.

BUT I CAN'T. I JUST CAN'T. SO...I'M GOING TO FIGHT HIM INSTEAD.

LIKE THAT SWIMMER SAID...

RMBL RMBL

SHOVE

I'M GOING TO BECOME THE CHAMPION OF EVERY POKÉMON CONTEST IN THE HOENN REGION!!!

YOU'RE NOT TAKING ME BACK HOME WITH YOU!!!

WHAT ?!

AND **THIS** IS THE BEST YOU CAN DO...?

REALLY ?

YOU'RE RIGHT ABOUT ONE THING... I BET YOU **CAN** ANTICIPATE ALL OF KIKI AND NANA'S MOVES, DAD.

BUT...

I'M THE ONE WHO TAUGHT YOU HOW TO USE THOSE MOVES.

IRON TAIL AND HYPER BEAM?

OH YEAH?

THIS IS POINT- LESS! ADMIT DEFEAT!

I KNOW WHAT YOU'RE GOING TO DO BEFORE YOU DO IT.

TNK TNK TNK

MUMU'S MUD SHOT !!!

THEY'RE FIGHTING ON THE ROOF-TOP?!

HEY! HEY!!

RMBL RMBL

WHAT IS GOING ON?!

ADVENTURE MAP

SAPPHIRE

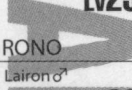 CHIC
Combusken♀
Lv25

 RONO
Lairon♂
Lv36

 LORRY
Wailord♂
Lv43

 PHADO
Donphan♂
Lv40

RUBY

 MUMU
Marshtomp♂

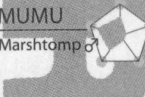 NANA
Mightyena♀

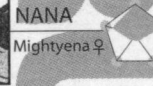 KIKI
Delcatty♀

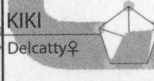 FEEBAS
Feebas♀

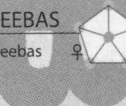

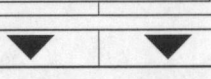

Route 109

Slateport City	Slateport City
Route 110	Route 118
Mauville City	Route 119
New Mauville	Weather Institute
Route 111	

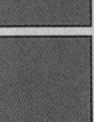
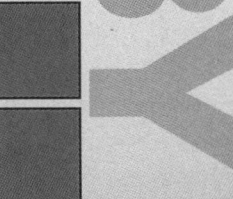

Stone Badge	Knuckle Badge	Dynamo Badge	Heat Badge

Balance Badge	Feather Badge	Mind Badge	Rain Badge
			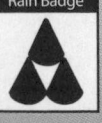

	Cool	Beauty	Cute	Smart	Tough
Normal	🎀	🎀	🎀	🎀	🎀
Super	🎀	🎀	🎀	🎀	🎀
Hyper					
Master					

● Chapter 210 ●
Hanging Around with Slaking II

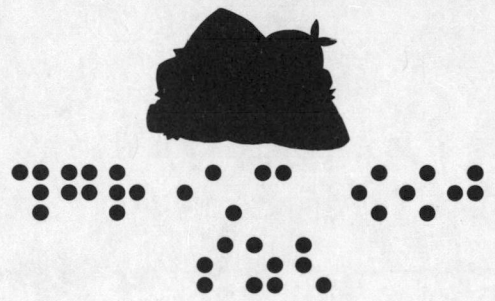

TNKTNKTNKTN

WIFS

HNNRGH!!

HE LURED ME IN FRONT OF THAT DRAIN INLET!!

NORMAN

RUBY

MUMU

HE HAD HIS MARSHTOMP ATTACK WITH MUD SHOT THROUGH THE DRAINPIPE!!

FOCUS PUNCH !!!

WHO D WHD WHD

BUT I HAVE THE ADVANTAGE!!

MUMU'S ATTACK AND VIGOROTH'S DEFENSE!! THEY PRETTY MUCH CANCEL EACH OTHER OUT...

NUTS! HE MANAGED TO MATCH MY ATTACKS!!

OW !!

CHU CHU CHU

TNK TNK TNK

THE WEATHER IS ON MY SIDE TODAY!!

THERE'S PLENTY OF RAIN AND MUD FOR MUMU TO USE FOR ITS ATTACKS!!

WE HAVE TO STOP THEM!!

WHO ARE YOU?!

YEP.

THOSE TWO ARE BATTLING, AREN'T THEY?

WHAT ARE YOU TALKING ABOUT?!

THAT'S RIGHT! THIS IS A FAMILY MATTER. LEAVE THEM BE.

GABBY, WE SHOULDN'T GET INVOLVED...

...NOT TO MENTION THE HELP OF A POWERFUL TRAINER LIKE NORMAN!!

...WE NEED INFORMATION FROM THE BOY WHO MET THEM PERSONALLY...

IF WE'RE SERIOUS ABOUT STOPPING THIS EVIL ORGANIZATION LURKING IN HOENN...

WE NEED THOSE TWO!!

ISN'T THERE SOME WAY TO STOP THOSE TWO FROM BATTLING?!

AND IF SOMETHING HAPPENS TO EITHER OF THEM, WE'LL LOSE THAT OPPORTUNITY!!

WEATHER POKÉMON
CASTFORM

CASTFORM CHANGE THEIR FORM AND TYPE DEPENDING ON THE WEATHER...

...BUT THEY ALSO HAVE THE POWER TO **CONTROL** THE WEATHER!

ABILITY: FORECAST

WAIT A MIN- UTE ...

THAT'S IT!!

PLEASE, CAST- FORM!!

PLEASE !!!

WE HAVE TO AT LEAST GIVE IT A TRY!

PLEASE! WE NEED YOUR HELP!!

RMBL

SNAG

RMBL RMBL RMB

HE MUSTN'T !!

THIS DOESN'T LOOK GOOD ...

RUBY'S ABOUT TO GO ALL-OUT WITH HIS NEXT ATTACK!!

...SOME MYSTERI-OUS EVIL HAS BEEN CREEPING INTO THE HOENN REGION!!

AND THOSE TWO ON THE ROOFTOP ARE THE ONES WHO CAN HELP US PREVENT THAT EVIL FROM SPREADING!!

PLEASE, CASTFORM... EVER SINCE PRESIDENT STONE WAS ATTACKED...

...LIKE PRESI-DENT STONE !!

I DON'T WANT ANY MORE VICTIMS ...

AAH ...

...YOUR POW-ERS !!

PLEASE! LEND ME...

DID WE MAKE IT IN TIME?

...SUNNY DAY...?

A ...

PANT PANT PANT

KRMBL

AAH!

PANT PANT PANT PANT PANT PANT

...READ THE LETTER HE WROTE YOU.

OH NO! THE GIFT FROM YOUR FATHER... YOU DIDN'T...

Happy Birthday
From Dad

OH, RUBY...

RUBY'S ROOM

FSSSS

BUT WE HAD OUR REASONS, YOU KNOW.

DEVON

...MOVE TO HOENN ON YOUR BIRTH-DAY.

MAYBE YOU DIDN'T UNDERSTAND WHY WE DECIDED TO...

WE WERE GOING TO HAVE DINNER TOGETHER TO CELEBRATE YOUR BIRTH-DAY AND OUR MOVE.

AND NOW THAT YOU'RE 11, YOUR FATHER WAS GOING TO GIVE YOU PERMISSION ...

...TO PURSUE YOUR DREAM OF COMPETING IN POKÉMON CONTESTS.

DAD ...!!

RUBY !!

● Chapter 211 ●
Hanging Around with Slaking III

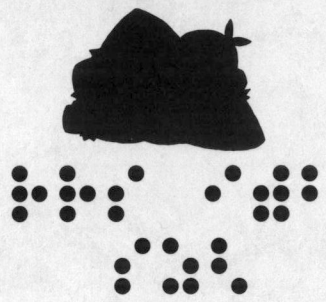

THOSE CONTESTS...

WHAT?! DID I HEAR YOU RIGHT JUST NOW...?!

SEVERAL MONTHS AGO...

PETALBURG GYM

I THINK WE OUGHT TO LET RUBY ENTER POKÉMON CONTESTS...

...IF THAT'S WHAT HE REALLY WANTS.

BUT HE'S GOING TO BE 11. HE'S OLD ENOUGH TO MAKE HIS OWN DECISIONS NOW.

THAT'S BECAUSE RUBY WAS STILL A CHILD.

BUT YOU'VE BEEN SO OPPOSED TO IT ALL THIS TIME!

BUT... HE HAS TO MAKE HIS OWN CHOICES ABOUT WHAT HE WANTS TO DO WITH HIS LIFE.

FRANKLY, I STILL WANT HIM TO TRAIN AND FIGHT POKÉMON BATTLES.

HE HASN'T NOTICED YET, BUT HE'S ACTUALLY EVEN BETTER AT POKÉMON BATTLING THAN I AM! IF HE'D FOCUS ON THAT...

WE CAN INVITE THE BIRCH FAMILY OVER AND HAVE DINNER TOGETHER TO CELEBRATE.

WHY DON'T WE MOVE TO HOENN IN TIME FOR RUBY'S BIRTHDAY?

FSSSS

...YOU'D HAD THE PATIENCE TO WAIT, RUBY...JUST A COUPLE MORE HOURS THAT DAY...

IF ONLY...

ALL RIGHT, DEAR.

I'LL TELL RUBY AT HIS BIRTHDAY DINNER.

ZOOP

KRASH

SMASH

SHAAA

HEY! YOU THERE!

NNGH!

SLIP

ARRGH...

THE RAIN IS MAKING THIS WORSE...

SLIP

CAST-FORM!

NOD

MOVE YOUR SUNLIGHT OVER HERE... RIGHT ABOVE ME!

I GET IT... SUNNY DAY ONLY CHANGES THE WEATHER IN A LIMITED AREA... SO HE HAD CASTFORM DRY THINGS OUT AROUND HIM!

PSSHH

PER-FECT!

GRIP!

SHLOOP

RSTL

THUNK

QUICK! WE'VE GOT TO GET DOWN THERE!!

WHAT HAP-PENED ?!

MY RUN-NING SHOES ...

THE PRESENT DAD GAVE ME FOR MY BIRTH-DAY ...

WZZZ

PANT

PANT

PANT

PANT

...OUR LIVES!

IT SAVED...

I HOPE YOU HAVE A GOOD EXCUSE FOR LEAVING YOUR GYM UNATTENDED FOR SUCH A LONG TIME WITHOUT NOTIFYING THE POKÉMON ASSOCIATION...

I CAME LOOKING FOR YOU BECAUSE TRAINERS HAVE BEEN COMPLAINING THAT YOU'RE NEVER IN WHEN THEY COME TO CHALLENGE YOU.

Uh-huh.

HA HA HA... I'M BEING SCOLDED FOR NOT BEING AT THE GYM BECAUSE I LEFT TO TRAIN MORE.

BOTH YOU AND FLANNERY HERE ARE STILL ROOKIE HOENN GYM LEADERS...

...AND I'M UNDER ORDERS TO SUPERVISE YOU TWO. I'M TAKING YOU BACK TO THE ASSOCIATION HEAD-QUARTERS WITH ME!!

YOU CAN EXPLAIN YOURSELF AFTER WE GET BACK!

I WANTED TO TELL YOU THAT YOU CAN PURSUE YOUR DREAM! YOU'RE FREE TO DO AS YOU WILL!!

YOU WENT OFF ON YOUR OWN... YOU WEREN'T PATIENT ENOUGH TO HEAR YOUR PARENTS OUT...

HEY !!

ONCE YOU DECIDE TO DO SOME- THING...

...GIVE IT YOUR ALL!!

BUT I EXPECT YOU TO DO YOUR BEST TO ACHIEVE YOUR GOAL!

AND DON'T FORGET TO CALL...YOUR **MOTHER** EVERY NOW AND THEN.

MM-HM.

BUT I'M SURE YOU'RE GOING TO NEED A LOT OF SUPPLIES TO DO THE JOB RIGHT.

I DON'T KNOW ANYTHING ABOUT POKÉMON CONTESTS. I HAVE NO IDEA WHAT YOU SEE IN THEM...

YOU SHOULD KEEP THEM IN A CASE.

YOU SCATTERED YOUR POKÉBLOCKS EVERYWHERE BACK IN SLATEPORT CITY.

Snff

HE'S NOT SUCH A BAD FATHER AFTER ALL.

UM...

See you, kiddo!

I'LL DRIVE YOU TO VERDAN-TURF TOWN.

YOU BETTER WIN SOME CON-TESTS!

YOU KNOW WHAT THIS MEANS, DON'T YOU...?

THANK YOU.

DAD....

OKAY, LET'S GET GOING!

SLAM

VROOM

SEE YOU!! TAKE CARE!!

AH!!

OH...

HA

HEY! HANG ON A MINUTE!!

WAIT!! HOW'D YOU LIKE TO START A FEEBAS FARM WITH ME...?!

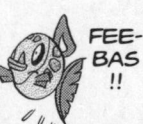

FEE- BAS !!

VROOM

...

YOU CAN GO WITH HIM IF YOU WANT TO, CAST-FORM.

!

144

LET'S ENTRUST THAT CAST-FORM TO HIS CARE.

HEY, TY... I'VE BEEN THINKING...

IT NEVER GOT ATTACHED TO US. BUT LOOK HOW ATTACHED IT'S GOTTEN TO RUBY AND HIS POKÉMON.

BUT SOMEBODY HAS TO TAKE CARE OF CASTFORM WHILE HE'S IN THE HOSPITAL, RIGHT?

FWIP FWIP

WHAT ARE YOU TALKING ABOUT, GABBY?! YOU CAN'T DO THAT WITHOUT PRESIDENT STONE'S PERMISSION!!

DON'T WORRY! AS LONG AS WE'RE WITH HIM, THE CASTFORM WILL ALWAYS BE IN SIGHT!

UH...

YOU MEAN YOU WANT US TO STICK WITH THIS KID?!

CASTFORM MUST SENSE SOMETHING ABOUT HIM!!

THAT'S WHY IT AGREED TO HELP HIM AND HIS FATHER!

DON'T SAY I DIDN'T WARN YOU!!

HMPH!!

VROOM

FWIP
FWIP

VROOM

SS DAYS LEFT UNTIL THE DEADLINE!

ADVENTURE MAP

SAPPHIRE

RUBY

CHIC
Combusken♀
Lv27

RONO
Lairon♂
Lv37

LORRY
Wailord♂
Lv43

PHADO
Donphan♂
Lv41

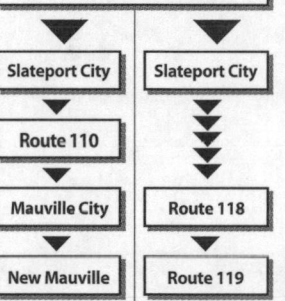

| Route 109 |
Slateport City	Slateport City
Route 110	
Mauville City	Route 118
New Mauville	Route 119
Route 111	Weather Institute

 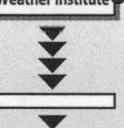

MUMU
Marshtomp♂

NANA
Mightyena♀

KIKI
Delcatty♀

FEEFEE
Feebas♀

CASTFORM
Castform♀

| Stone Badge | Knuckle Badge | Dynamo Badge | Heat Badge |
| Balance Badge | Feather Badge | Mind Badge | Rain Badge |

		Cool	Beauty	Cute	Smart	Tough
Super	Normal					
Hyper						
Master						

● Chapter 212 ●
Bubble Bubble Toil and Azumarill I

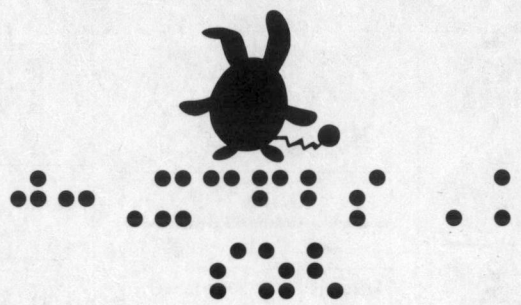

The Fourth Chapter

FWOOOF

FLAMETHROWER!!

WON-
DERFUL,
FLAN-
NERY!!

PUFFF

KRKL-KRKL

THAT'S THE 149TH CHALLENGER YOU'VE DEFEATED SINCE YOU BECAME A GYM LEADER... THAT'S MORE THAN ENOUGH TO COMPENSATE FOR THE TROUBLE YOU'VE CAUSED!

YOU'RE A ROOKIE GYM LEADER, BUT YOUR BATTLES ARE LIKE THOSE OF A SKILLED VETERAN!

...THIS GIRL.

SHE BEAT ROXANNE, BRAWLY **AND** WATTSON...

WINONA, I'VE HEARD ABOUT...

...THAT'S THREE TRAINERS— AND THREE BADGES— IN A VERY SHORT TIME!

HER NAME IS SAP-PHIRE.

I BETTER GO OUT TO TRAIN FOR A BIT!!

THE NEXT PLACE SHE'LL VISIT IS VERY LIKELY TO BE HERE ...

ISN'T IT OBVIOUS?

MT. CHIMNEY

LAVARIDGE TOWN

MAUVILLE CITY

I'VE HEARD OF HER TOO. WHY THE INTEREST?

COME AND CHAL-LENGE ME!!

OKAY !!

...SAPPHIRE!!

I'M READY FOR YOU ...

YOU KNOW HER, DON'T YOU?

COULD YOU TELL US...

DID YOU JUST SAY "SAP-PHIRE"?

SAP-PHIRE ?

...MORE ABOUT HER ?!

OOOH.

THE WHOLE AREA'S BURNIN' HOT BECAUSE OF THE HEAT FROM THAT VOLCANO.

MT. CHIMNEY ...

THIS PLACE LOOKS MIGHTY GRAND CLOSE UP, EH?

FSSST

RUN!!

HUH?

RMBL

MISS FLANNERY, THE INTEL YOU GAVE US ABOUT SAPPHIRE COMING TO LAVARIDGE TOWN HAS TURNED OUT TO BE MOST HELPFUL.

YOU'RE HERE, SAPPHIRE.

I MUST REMEMBER TO THANK SHELLY AND AMBER FOR CAPTURING YOU.

...THAT GUY FROM PETALBURG WOODS!!

OH! HE'S...

JUST LIKE SHE SAID YOU WOULD BE.

MMPH! MMPH!*

*RUN! RUN!

I WON'T LET YOU GET AWAY!!

DID YOU SERIOUSLY THINK I WOULDN'T BE ABLE TO GET UP HERE?!

PFFSSt

GRIT

I'M SO GLAD WE MEET AGAIN. AND NOW...

LONG TIME NO SEE.

NOT AT ALL. AS A MATTER OF FACT, I WANTED YOU TO COME HERE.

OPEN

KACHAK

HOW COULD THEY DO SOMETHING LIKE THIS ...?

YOU'RE NOT GONNA GET AWAY WITH THIS!

USIN' SOMEONE I DON'T EVEN KNOW AS BAIT?!!

SPLASH SPLASH

HA HA HA... AND THERE'S MORE TO COME.

WHOA!!

WOOSH

AND THE WATER WILL JUST KEEP COMING ...

THIS CABLE CAR IS COMPLETELY SEALED. ABSOLUTELY AIRTIGHT.

SPLASH SPLASH

...UNDERWATER, ISN'T IT?

KIND OF HARD TO BREATHE ...

SP L SH SPL SH SPL SH

HA HA HA HA HA ...

...FOR YOU... GURGH !!

BUT IT'S THE SAME ...

PLUNK

!!

PUFF PUFF

I HAVE A WAY AROUND THAT PROBLEM.

DON'T WORRY ABOUT ME.

BUT YOU KNEW THAT, RIGHT?

THEY MAKE AIR BALLOONS TO SAVE OTHER POKÉMON AND PEOPLE FROM DROWNING.

AREA | CRY | SIZE | ???

No056 Azumarill
Aqua Rabbit Pokémon
Height: 2'07''
Weight: 62.8lbs.

Azumarill can make balloons out of air. It makes these air balloons if it spots a drowning Pokémon. The air balloons enable the Pokémon in trouble to breathe.

THANKS TO MY AZUMARILL.

HMMMMGH!!!

BUBBL BUBBL

NO?

BUBBL BUBBL BUBBL

RMB

RMBL

RMBLRMBL

GOOD
!!

EVERY-
THING
IS
READY
!!

...TO
PERMA-
NENTLY
PUT A STOP
TO THE
VOLCANIC
ACTIVITY
OF THIS
MOUNTAIN
!!!

AND
NOW
IT'S
UP TO
TEAM
AQUA...

● Chapter 213 ●
Bubble Bubble Toil and Azumarill II

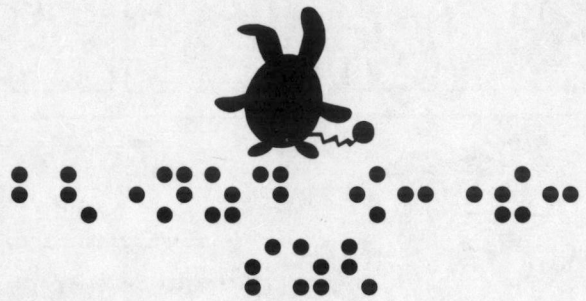

The Fourth Chapter

RMBL

HMMMGH!!

LUNGE

HAR HAR HAR HAR !!

GRRRGH...

SLASH

URRGH!!

TANG BOM THO ATK

RONO, PLEASE!!

I'LL BE DONE FOR IF I GET BITTEN!!

RUP RUP RUP

...YOU'VE AVOIDED THE WORST?!

!!

YOU'VE BROKEN ALL OF SHARPEDO'S FANGS.

OOH, IRON DEFENSE. NOT BAD.

BUT DO YOU IMAGINE THAT MEANS ...

SHARPE-DO'S FANGS GROW BACK AS SOON AS THEY BREAK OFF!!

No098 Sharpedo
Brutal Pokémon
Height: 5'11''
Weight: 195.8lbs.

Nicknamed "the bully of the sea," Sharpedo is widely feared. Its cruel fangs grow back immediately if they snap off. Just one of these Pokémon can thoroughly tear apart a supertanker.

SO CLOSE, AND YET...

...THE FANGS WILL JUST KEEP GROW-ING BACK!!

NO MATTER HOW MANY TIMES YOU MANAGE TO DEFLECT SHARPEDO'S ATTACKS WITH YOUR LAIRON...

TCH...

IT'S OVER!

GRN

BUMP

BY NOW, MATT MUST HAVE GOTTEN RID OF THAT LITTLE GIRL.
NOW WE CAN GET BACK TO WHAT'S **REALLY** IMPORTANT...
... FINISHING UP AT THE VOLCANO!
RMBL
RMBL
EVERYTHING'S FALLING INTO PLACE.
RMBL
RMBL
HEH HEH HEH HEH...
IT'S BEEN FOUR MINUTES SINCE THE CABLE CAR STARTED MOVING.
AS LONG AS SHELLY DOESN'T MESS UP...
HOW'S IT GOING, SHELLY?
EVERYTHING'S GOING ACCORDING TO PLAN, AMBER.
I'M AT METEOR FALLS. YES, I MET UP WITH HIM.
RMBL RMBL RMBL
HE'S RIGHT BESIDE ME.

FOR THE OPPORTUNITY TO DO RESEARCH ON THESE MINERALS HERE WITH YOU.

YES, RIGHT! THANKS FOR EVERYTHING...

ISN'T THAT RIGHT, PROFESSOR COZMO?

THANK YOU.

TEAM AQUA WILL ALWAYS BE RIGHT BEHIND YOU TO FUND YOUR WORK.

WE WANT A TALENTED MAN LIKE YOU TO BE ABLE TO CONCENTRATE ON YOUR RESEARCH WITHOUT HAVING TO WORRY ABOUT YOUR BUDGET.

NO NEED TO THANK US.

AND FOR FUNDING MY RESEARCH TO BOOT!

OH, SURE.

ER, PROFESSOR COZMO... I DON'T MEAN TO RUSH YOU, BUT...COULD YOU BRING THAT METEOR YOU JUST DUG UP WITH YOU?

THANK YOU VERY MUCH.

YOUR ORGANIZATION UNDERSTANDS THAT. AND YOU'RE MAKING A GREAT EFFORT TO PROTECT IT AND THOSE WHO LIVE IN IT. I APPLAUD YOU.

THE SEA IS THE SOURCE OF ALL LIFE ON THIS PLANET.

PHEW!

GR IN

SPLISH

WHAT'S THAT SOUND?!

HA HA HA... MY FIRST TASK...

...SINCE MY PRO-MOTION...

OH

SPLASH

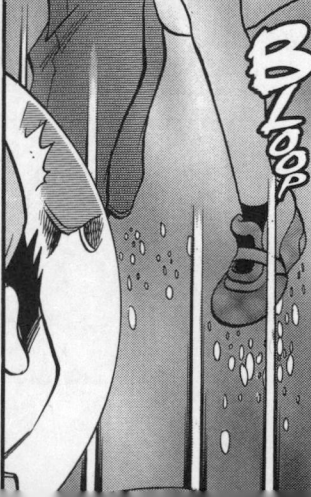

BLOOP

FSSSS

KRAKRA

THE WATER LEVEL IS GOING DOWN!!

IMPOSSIBLE!!

FOOOOSH

BUT THAT WASN'T MY ONLY AIM...

YOU THOUGHT I WAS ONLY PROTECTIN' MYSELF WHEN I USED RONO TO STOP SHARPEDO'S ATTACK, DIDN'TCHA?

HOW?!

PANT PANT PANT

...AND USED 'EM TO PUNCH A HOLE IN THE WINDOW!!

I GRABBED THE BROKEN FANGS FLOATIN' IN THE WATER— WITHOUT LETTIN' YOU SEE...

CHHHTING

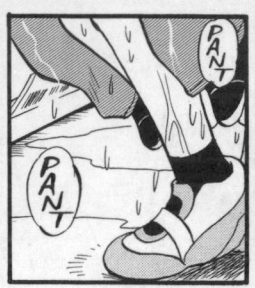

PANT
PANT

UHH

URGH
...

BOING

PANT
PANT
PANT

TMP

YOU'RE JUST LIKE EVERYONE SAID—AN AMAZING TRAINER!

I'M SO SORRY ...

...I TOLD THEM ABOUT YOU...

PANT

PANT

COUGH, COUGH, COUGH!

HANG IN THERE.

THANKS —

PANT

I DON'T HAVE TIME TO SIT AROUND...

PANT

PANT

THEY'RE PROBABLY GOING TO DO SOMETHING TERRIBLE TO THE VOLCANO!!

I'M A GYM LEADER!!

AND I WON'T LET THEM GET AWAY WITH ANY FUNNY BUSINESS IN MY TOWN!!

PANT

PANT

CLIMB...

WHAT-CHA GONNA DO NOW?!

SOME SORT OF PLAN ...

DO YOU REMEM-BER WHAT HE SAID?

THE GYM LEADER OF LAVARIDGE TOWN!!

I'M FLANNERY!

A... GYM LEADER ?!

OH!

I THINK IT WOULD BE A GOOD IDEA FOR US TO STICK TOGETHER!

YOU KNOW...IF THAT CABLE CAR GETS TO THE TOP SOMEONE'S GONNA NOTICE THAT...

I'LL GO WITH YA!!

...THAT CREEP DIDN'T GET RID OF ME!

TMP

YOU HAVE A POKÉMON THAT CAN FLY?

ON A POKÉMON OF COURSE.

FLY? HOW?

BUT WE AIN'T EXACTLY IN TIP-TOP CONDITION, SO...LET'S FLY UP TO THE PEAK!

174

RIGHT HERE!

WHERE IS IT...?

I USUALLY LET IT ROAM FREE. I DON'T LIKE TO KEEP IT INSIDE A POKÉ BALL.

IT'S MY DAD'S. HE LENT IT TO ME. SAID I COULD USE IT WHENEVER I NEEDED A LIFT IN THE SKY.

AIN'T MINE.

FWEEEE

RSTL RSTL

● Chapter 214 ●
Assaulted by Pelipper I

The Fourth Chapter

AMBER, ONE OF THE THREE TEAM AQUA ADMINS— OTHERWISE KNOWN AS THE SSS.

EH? AND YOU ARE...?

PHEW!

NICE TO MEET YOU. IT'S TERRIBLY HOT UP HERE NEAR THE CRATER, ISN'T IT?

AH!! WEL-COME TO OUR EXPERI-MENT.

FZ Z Z Z Z Z

HERE WE ARE, PRO-FESSOR COZMO.

OH! THEN **THIS** MUST BE THE MACHINE YOU TOLD ME ABOUT...

IT'S *HUGE* !!!

THE ONE THAT WILL TEMPORARILY HALT THE MOUNTAIN'S VOLCANIC ACTIVITY SO WE CAN RAISE THE SEA LEVEL NEAR HERE.

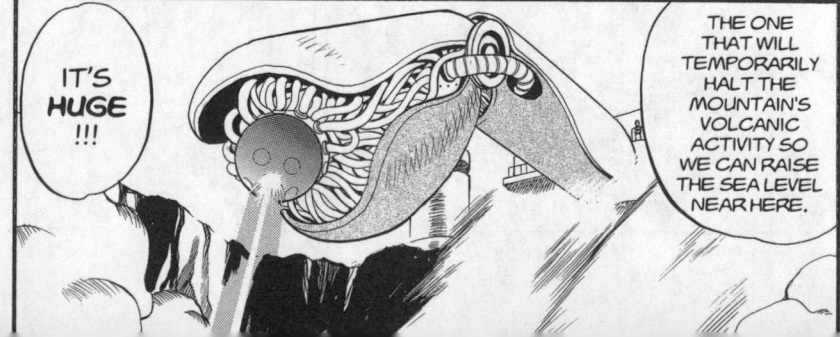

WE DON'T KNOW THE REASON, BUT WE MUST PUT A STOP TO IT. THE SEA MUST BE PROTECTED!

ACCORDING TO OUR DATA, THE HOENN REGION SEA LEVELS HAVE BEEN DECLINING RAPIDLY IN THE PAST YEAR.

MT. CHIMNEY IS AN ACTIVE VOLCANO, AND THE MACHINE DOESN'T HAVE ENOUGH POWER TO CONTROL IT.

HOWEVER, THERE IS ONE SMALL ISSUE...

THE EXPERIMENT IS ALREADY UNDERWAY.

MY! WHAT A WONDERFUL ORGANIZATION YOU HAVE!!

OF COURSE! MY PLEASURE!

WE NEED THE METEOR YOU DUG UP, AS WELL AS YOUR UNIQUE TECHNOLOGY TO EXTRACT ITS ENERGY!

THAT'S WHERE YOU COME IN, PROFESSOR COZMO!

SO THIS IS...

KLK

...THE METEOR-ITE THAT FELL FROM SPACE...

THE BLUE-PRINTS YOU PROVIDED WERE VERY HELPFUL. WE'VE ALREADY ATTACHED YOUR DEVICE TO THE MACHINE.

FFFSSSSST

TCK
TCK

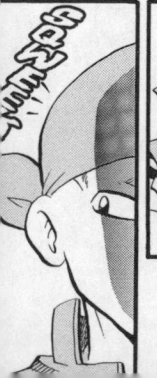

EXCELLENT. IT WILL CONVERT THE ENERGY FROM THE METEORITE.

AQUA ADMIN AMBER— WE'VE GOT TROUBLE!!

SKWEK

EH?

MATT!!

A RIVAL ORGANIZATION IS BENT ON INTERFERING WITH US, PROFESSOR COZMO!!

WHAT'S GOING ON?!

NNGH! HE FAILED TO GET RID OF SAPPHIRE!!

AI-IEEE!!

YES. THERE ARE THREE SSS TEAM AQUA ADMINS IN ALL, AND EACH OF US HAD A MISSION TODAY...

A... RIVAL ORGANIZATION?!

THEY'RE COMPLETELY UNPREDICTABLE! I HAVE NO IDEA WHAT THEY MIGHT DO TO YOU IF THEY CATCH YOU!!

PROFESSOR COZMO, IT'S TOO DANGEROUS HERE!! MY GUESS IS OUR ENEMIES ARE HEADED FOR THE MOUNTAIN'S PEAK!!

BUT IT APPEARS HIS NEGOTIATIONS WERE UNSUCCESSFUL!! JUST LOOK AT WHAT THEY DID TO HIM...!!

MY JOB WAS TO CARRY OUT THE EXPERIMENT. SHELLY'S WAS TO BRING YOU HERE...

...AND MATT'S WAS TO TRY AND REASON WITH THIS OPPOSITION GROUP.

EEK!!

WILL DO! PLEASE COME WITH ME, PROFESSOR!!

SHELLY! YOU PROTECT PROFESSOR COZMO AND CHARGE THE MACHINE WITH THE ENERGY FROM THE METEORITE!

I'LL TAKE CARE OF THE OPPOSITION!!

PULL

WHERE ARE THEY...?!

COME OUT, PELIPPER!!

FLAP FLAP

BOM

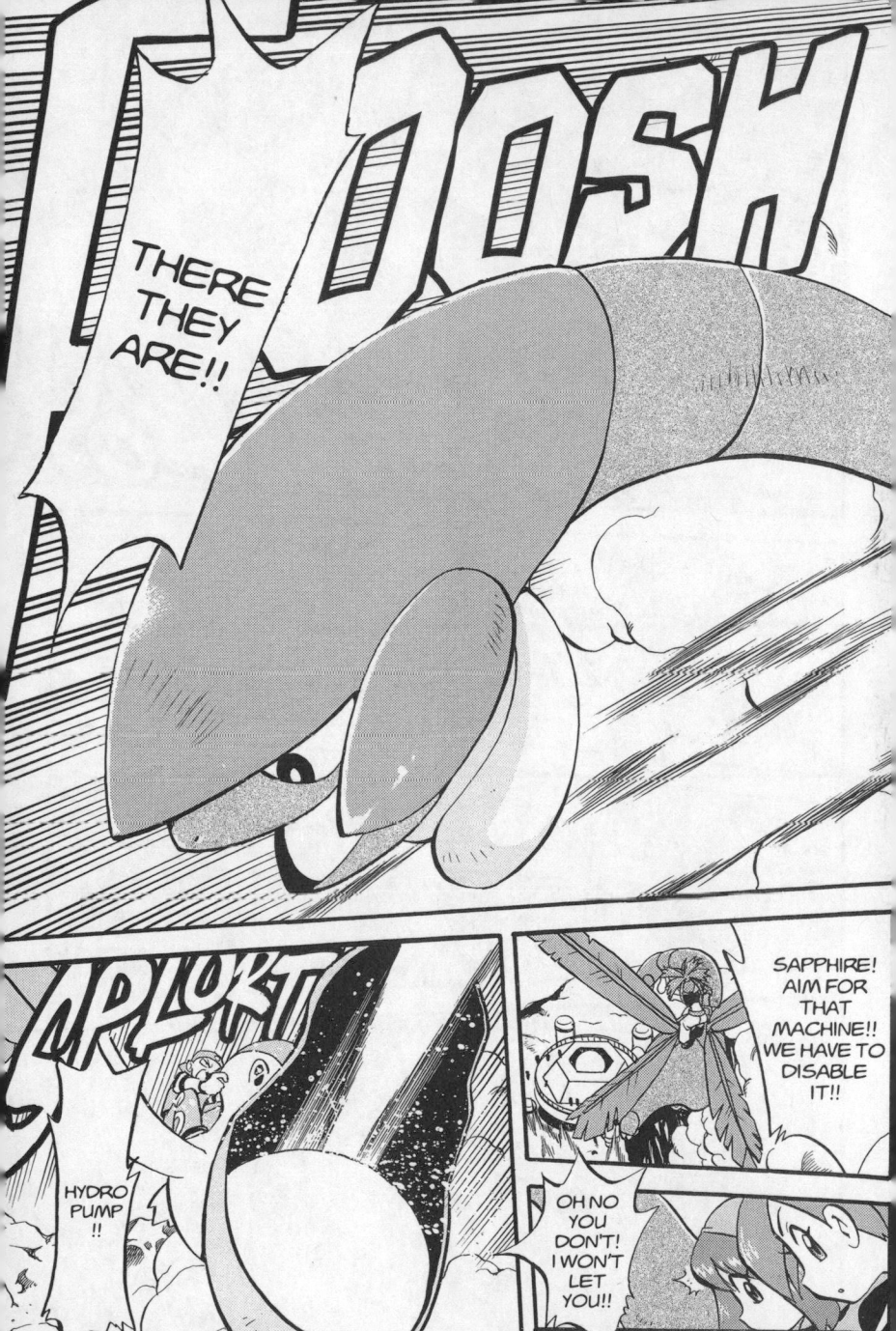

THAT WON'T STOP US!!!

SPLOOSH

OKAY!!

HURRY! YOU HAVE TO SET EVERYTHING UP QUICKLY—IN CASE THEY DEFEAT AMBER!

PROFESSOR COZMO, THAT'S THEM!! THEY'RE AFTER THE METEORITE— AND THIS MACHINE!

HURRY, PROFESSOR COZMO !!

URGH!!

TAP TAP TAP

TAP TAP

SAPPHIRE! IT'S OKAY! WE'RE WINNING! LET'S MAKE SHORT WORK OF HIM AND THEN GO BREAK THAT MACHINE INTO LITTLE PIECES!!

SOME-THING'S NOT RIGHT!

WHAT ?!

I'M TRYIN'!! BUT I CAN'T!

IT SEEMS LIKE WE HAVE THE UPPER HAND, BUT...HE KEEPS ATTACKIN' ME AT JUST THE RIGHT MOMENT SO I CAN'T GET CLOSE TO THE MACHINE.

I DON'T KNOW WHY HE WOULD DO THAT, BUT...

IT'S LIKE HE'S PRE-TENDIN' HE'S HAVIN' A HARD TIME OR SOME-THIN'...

TROPPY'S MOST POWERFUL MOVE! IT NEVER MISSES!

...HE WON'T BE ABLE TO PRETEND ANYTHIN' WHEN I DO THIS!

ROAR

TAKE THAT !!

FLAP

IT REPELLED MAGICAL LEAF?!

THANKS TO YOU, HE DID. AND NOW THE MACHINE IS CHARGED UP AND...

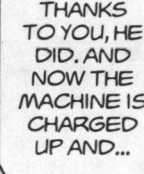

I WAS JUST TRYING TO TRICK THAT STUPID SCIENTIST INTO BELIEVING OUR STORY.

AHA HA HA HA HA... WE DID IT!

BUT I WASN'T TRYING TO FOOL *YOU.*

YOU'RE VERY CLEVER.

...THIS MOUNTAIN'S VOLCANIC ACTIVITY HAS COMPLETELY CEASED!!!

HSSSSSSSS

FHWZZ

THE TOWN OF HOT SPRINGS
LAVARIDGE TOWN

HEY! IS THE HOT SPRING GETTING COLD ALL OF A SUDDEN?!

AH-CHOO!!

POKE MON CENTER

THE HOT SPRINGS HAVE GONE COLD!!

WHAT'S GOING ON?!

THIS IS RIDICU-LOUS!

WHAT THE...?!

THE HOT SPRINGS ARE ALWAYS HOT AND STEAMY! THEY'RE WARMED BY MT. CHIMNEY!

WOOSH

I'VE NEVER HEARD OF THIS HAPPENING IN THE HISTORY OF LAVARIDGE TOWN!

IT'S NOT JUST THE HOT SPRINGS!

THE WHOLE...

AND NO ASH!

HEY, LOOK...! THERE'S NO SMOKE COMING FROM THE VOLCANO!

...IS GETTING CHILLY!!

...TOWN...

GRIN

THE CESSATION OF MT. CHIMNEY'S VOLCANIC ACTIVITY...

...HAS HAD A DRASTIC INFLUENCE NOT ONLY ON LAVARIDGE TOWN, BUT DEEP BENEATH THE SURFACE OF THE ENTIRE HOENN REGION!

THE BALANCE OF ENERGY HAS BEEN DISRUPTED...

THIS IMBALANCE IS SLOWLY BUT SURELY AWAKENING ANCIENT CREATURES SLUMBERING IN THE UNDERGROUND DEPTHS...

BUBBL BUBBL

RMBL RMBL

49 DAYS LEFT UNTIL THE DEADLINE!

TO BE CONTINUED...

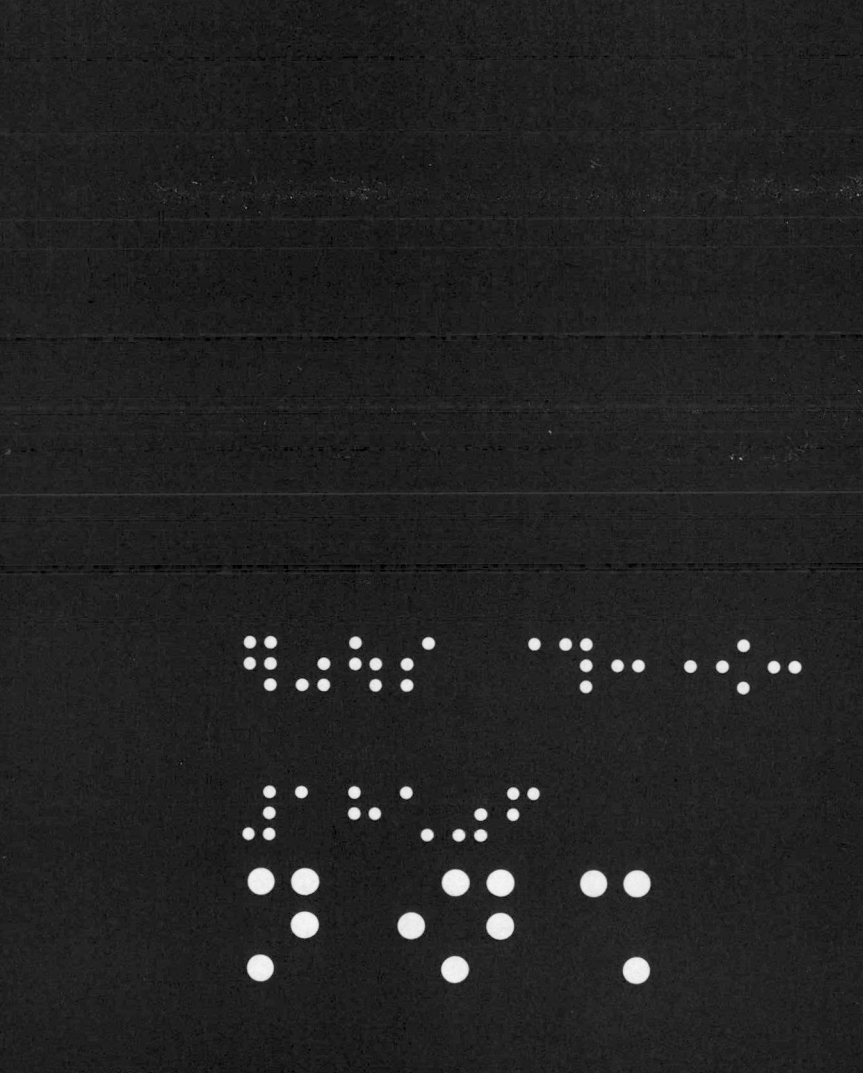

NEXT VOLUME!

THE BALANCE OF ENERGY IN THE HOENN REGION BEGINS TO COLLAPSE AFTER THE INCIDENT AT MT. CHIMNEY. THE STRONGEST EFFECT IS FELT DEEP BENEATH THE GROUND! HOW WILL RUBY AND SAPPHIRE BECOME INVOLVED...?

POKéMON ADVENTURES RUBY & SAPPHIRE Volume 18!

Enemies attacking one after the other!!

Two organizations that stand in the way!!

Will Ruby and Sapphire...

...manage to complete their journey?!!

Illustration Gallery

● Title ●

New Adventure

● Date drawn ●

Around November 2002

● Title ●

The New Heroes!!

● Date drawn ●

Around November 2002

● Title ●

Let's Go to the New World!

● Date drawn ●

Around December 2002

● Title ●

Mad Dash!!

●Date drawn●

Around September 2003

● Title ●

Run Like the Wind!!

●Date drawn●

Around December 2003

Illustration Gallery

● Title ●

Together!

● Date drawn ●

Around November 2003

THE GYM LEADERS OF HOENN

TEAM AQUA AND TEAM MAGMA ARE ABOUT TO MAKE THEIR MOVE. HOW WILL THE GYM LEADERS THWART THEM?

The rise of the ancient Pokémon draws near! What will the role of each town's Gym Leader be...?!

THE GYM LEADERS HAVE LEARNED OF THE PRESENCE OF BOTH OF THESE TWO EVIL ORGANIZATIONS, NOW THAT FLANNERY HAS TANGLED WITH TEAM AQUA. THE STORY OF THE INCIDENT AT MT. CHIMNEY WILL BE QUICKLY PASSED ON TO THE OTHER GYM LEADERS.

....

WITH THE DISRUPTION OF THE BALANCE OF ENERGY, THE HOENN REGION IS IN CRISIS. NOW IS THE TIME FOR THE GYM LEADERS TO JOIN FORCES TO PROTECT THE REGION! LET'S TAKE A CLOSER LOOK AT THEM...

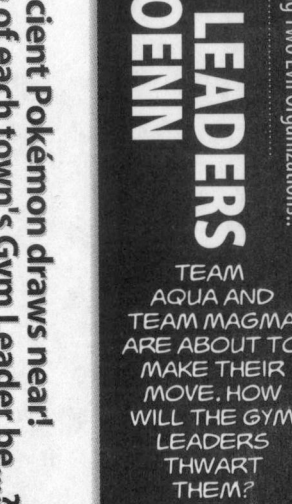

AQUA

MAGMA

THE ROCK-LOVING HONORS STUDENT!

ROXANNE

RUSTBORO CITY POKÉMON GYM LEADER

....

SHE DISPLAYED HER DEEP KNOWLEDGE OF POKÉMON WHEN FACING SAPPHIRE, KNOWLEDGE THAT COULD BE A GREAT WEAPON AGAINST TEAM AQUA AND TEAM MAGMA. ON THE OTHER HAND, SHE MIGHT NOT BE GOOD AT WORKING WITH OTHERS AS A TEAM. WILL THAT LEAD TO PROBLEMS...?

....

▲ HER MAIN POKÉMON IS NOSEPASS, A VERY DEFENSIVE POKÉMON.

EXPERTISE
ROCK TYPE

GYM BADGE

STONE BADGE

FLANNERY

**LAVARIDGE TOWN
POKÉMON
GYM LEADER**

FLANNERY IS A STRAIGHT-FORWARD PERSON AND A HARD WORKER. SHE WAS THE FIRST GYM LEADER TO FALL VICTIM TO ONE OF TEAM AQUA'S SCHEMES, AND SHE IS CURRENTLY FIGHTING AGAINST THEM. SHE MAY BE A ROOKIE, BUT HER DETERMINATION TO CARRY ON WITH HER RESPONSI-BILITIES IS THE STRONGEST OF ANY GYM LEADER.

ITS FLAMES HAVE DEFEATED MANY CHALLENGERS. WILL THEY ALSO DEFEAT THE ENEMY...?

EXPERTISE

FIRE TYPE

GYM BADGE

HEAT
BADGE

WATTSON

**MAUVILLE CITY
POKÉMON
GYM LEADER**

THE TRUE SKILLS OF WATTSON, AN ELECTRIC-TYPE POKÉMON EXPERT, HAVE YET TO BE REVEALED. BUT HE ISN'T JUST AN ORDINARY JOKESTER. THIS MAN LOVES HIS TOWN AND ITS CHILDREN AND WILL NEVER ALLOW EVIL TO PREVAIL!

WATTSON'S ELECTRIKE WAS A BIG HELP AT NEW MAUVILLE. LOOK FORWARD TO SEEING ITS EVOLV-ED FORM SOON!

EXPERTISE

ELECTRIC TYPE

GYM BADGE

DYNAMO
BADGE

BRAWLY

**DEWFORD TOWN
POKÉMON
GYM LEADER**

BRAWLY, THE MASTER OF THE "SOFT AND FLEXIBLE FIGHTING STYLE," MAY SEEM LIGHT-HEARTED, BUT HE HAS SERIOUS SKILLS! WE'LL SEE HOW THEY'VE IMPROVED WHEN HE REAPPEARS IN THE STORY AFTER HIS TIME AT TRAINING CAMP.

HARIYAMA IS A WALL OF MUSCLE. NO ENEMY CAN GET THROUGH IT.

EXPERTISE

FIGHTING TYPE

GYM BADGE

KNUCKLE
BADGE

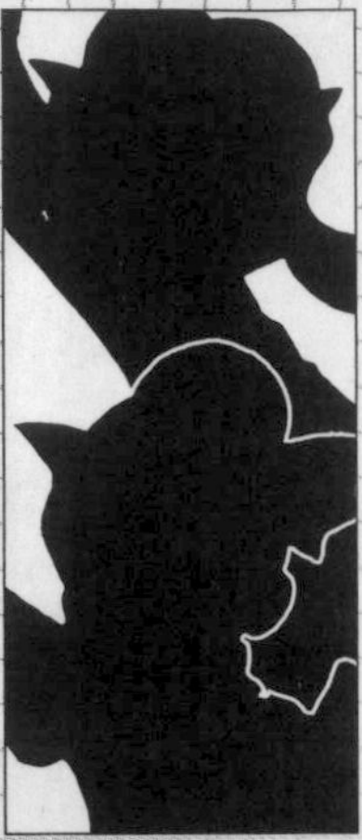

THE MYSTIC COMBINATION!

TATE & LIZA

MOSSDEEP CITY POKÉMON GYM LEADER

A UNIQUE GYM LEADER DUO WHO MANAGE ONE GYM TOGETHER. TATE AND LIZA'S SKILLS ARE AS YET UNKNOWN, BUT APPARENTLY THEY ARE UNDEFEATABLE IN A DOUBLE BATTLE.

◀▼ THEY USE A POKÉMON DUO AS WELL, WHO DISPLAY PERFECT TEAMWORK.

EXPERTISE

PSYCHIC TYPE

GYM BADGE

MIND BADGE

THE FLYING-TYPE POKÉMON TRAINER TAKES FLIGHT INTO THE WORLD!

WINONA

FORTREE CITY POKÉMON GYM LEADER

THE POKÉMON ASSOCIATION CHOSE HER AS THE LEADER AND SUPERVISOR OF THE OTHER GYM LEADERS BECAUSE OF HER GREAT SKILL. WINONA IS A WOMAN OF INTEGRITY. HOW WILL SHE USE HER LEADERSHIP TO FACE DOWN THESE GREAT EVILS?

◀ AS A TRAINER SPECIALIZING IN FLYING-TYPE POKÉMON, SHE FACES HER ENEMIES IN THE AIR.

EXPERTISE

FLYING TYPE

GYM BADGE

FEATHER BADGE

A MAN IN PURSUIT OF POWER!

NORMAN

PETALBURG CITY POKÉMON GYM LEADER

THE STRONGEST GYM LEADER, AND RUBY'S FATHER. HE HAS EXCEPTIONAL SKILLS. NORMAN IS A LONE WOLF WHO IS ALWAYS STRIVING TO INCREASE HIS STRENGTH. HE WOULD BE A GREAT HELP IN FIGHTING THE TWO EVIL SYNDICATES—IF HE EVER AGREED TO.

GRR
◀ UNMATCHED POWER. CRUSHES EVERYTHING AROUND IT.

EXPERTISE

NORMAL TYPE

GYM BADGE

BALANCE BADGE

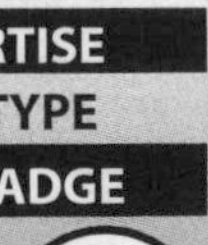

KEYWORDS

POKÉMON ASSOCIATION

THE POKÉMON ASSOCIATION CHOOSES AND APPOINTS GYM LEADERS. THE GYM LEADERS ACT UPON ORDERS FROM THE ASSOCIATION—AS LONG AS THEY ARE IN LINE WITH THEIR BELIEFS. NOW THAT THEY'VE LEARNED OF THE EXISTENCE OF TEAM AQUA AND TEAM MAGMA, HOW WILL THE POKÉMON ASSOCIATION DEAL WITH THEM?!

THE ▼ POKÉMON ASSOCIATION EXERTS ITS INFLUENCE THROUGH WATTSON AND WINONA. THESE TWO GYM LEADERS GUIDE THE OTHERS.

THOSE KIDS HAD PIZZAZZ. I DON'T SEE ANYTHING WRONG WITH GIVING THEM BADGES.

BY THE AUTHORITY VESTED IN ME BY THE POKÉMON ASSOCIATION, I MAY GIVE OUT BADGES AS I SEE FIT.

CAREER

THE LENGTH OF A GYM LEADER'S CAREER IS PROPORTIONATE TO THEIR INFLUENCE UPON THE PEOPLE AROUND THEM. OBVIOUSLY THE OPINIONS OF TRAINERS WHO HAVE BEEN GYM LEADERS FOR A LONG TIME CARRY GREATER WEIGHT, AND THE ASSOCIATION HAS A LOT OF FAITH IN THEM.

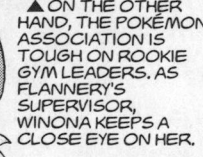

THAT'S THE FIFTH GYM CHALLENGER YOU'VE DEFEATED SINCE YOU BECAME A GYM LEADER... THAT'S MORE THAN ENOUGH TO COMPENSATE FOR THE TROUBLE YOU'VE CAUSED!

YOU'RE A ROOKIE GYM LEADER, BUT YOUR BATTLES ARE LIKE THOSE OF A SKILLED VETERAN!

▲ ON THE OTHER HAND, THE POKÉMON ASSOCIATION IS TOUGH ON ROOKIE GYM LEADERS. AS FLANNERY'S SUPERVISOR, WINONA KEEPS A CLOSE EYE ON HER.

NORMAN IS ◄ ALSO A ROOKIE GYM LEADER. WHY WAS HE UNABLE TO BECOME A GYM LEADER UNTIL NOW...? HMM...

WALLACE

SOOTOPOLIS CITY POKÉMON GYM LEADER

WALLACE IS ALSO A MYSTERY FOR NOW, A UNIQUE HOENN GYM LEADER WHO HAS SOMETHING TO DO WITH THE RISE OF ANCIENT POKÉMON. KEEP A CLOSE EYE ON HIM!

◄ A SHAPE WHICH SYMBOLIZES LOVE.

EXPERTISE
WATER TYPE

GYM BADGE
RAIN BADGE

Message from
Hidenori Kusaka

Things have become very convenient with the development of the personal computer. When I started this work, I wrote the story on manuscript paper by hand, but now I type away on my keyboard every day. And when I need to turn in my work, I send it by email. But when we become too dependent on such conveniences, I worry our work might lose its liveliness. Manga is something that is created by hand, so it's like an organic life-form... I especially feel this way when I'm editing the graphic novels.

Message from
Satoshi Yamamoto

The Ruby/Sapphire story arc is already in its third volume! The main event of this volume is obviously the family conflict between Ruby and Norman!! But personally, I'm more fond of the storyline with the Swimmer and the Trick Master. As a matter of fact, I think the Swimmer is the other main character in the family conflict. (What? You don't agree...?)

More Adventures Coming Soon...

Ruby arrives in Verdanturf Town ready to participate in his first Hoenn region Pokémon Contest. It looks like his dream of becoming the Pokémon Contest Champion is finally back on track! But he gets sidetracked yet again when he is asked to rescue a Trainer from a Rusturf Tunnel collapse. Could Team Magma be behind this latest *un*natural disaster...?

Then, both Ruby and Sapphire begin a losing streak...

Meanwhile, the Hoenn Gym Leaders can't agree... which group is evil? Team Magma or Team Aqua...or both?!

AVAILABLE NOW!

When Destruction Arises, Can Life Prevail?

POKÉMON

POKÉMON THE MOVIE

DIANCIE AND THE COCOON OF DESTRUCTION

Can Ash and his friends help Diancie discover its true power,
stop Yveltal's rampage, and save the Diamond Domain?

IN STORES NATIONWIDE

VISIT viz.com FOR MORE INFORMATION

©2015 Pokémon. ©1998–2014 PIKACHU PROJECT.
TM, ®, and character names are trademarks of Nintendo.

A NEW MEGA ADVENTURE!

THE SERIES XY

Ash Ketchum's journey continues in **Pokémon the Series: XY** as he arrives in the Kalos region, a land bursting with beauty, full of new Pokémon to be discovered!

24 ACTION-PACKED EPISODES!

Pick up **Pokémon the Series: XY** today!

IN STORES NATIONWIDE

visit **viz.com** for more information

viz media

The Pokémon Company INTERNATIONAL

TV Y7 FV

DVD VIDEO

©2015 Pokémon.
©1997-2014 Nintendo, Creatures, GAME FREAK, TV Tokyo, ShoPro, JR Kikaku. TM, ® Nintendo.

POKéMON™
ADVENTURES
HeartGold & SoulSilver

Story by HIDENORI KUSAKA
Art by SATOSHI YAMAMOTO

In this **two-volume** thriller, troublemaker Gold and feisty Silver must team up again to find their old enemy Lance and the Legendary Pokémon Arceus!

Available now!

www.viz.com

© 2013 Pokémon.
© 1995-2013 Nintendo/Creatures Inc./GAME FREAK inc.
TM and ® and character names are trademarks of Nintendo.
POCKET MONSTERS SPECIAL © 1997 Hidenori KUSAKA, Satoshi YAMAMOTO/SHOGAKUKAN

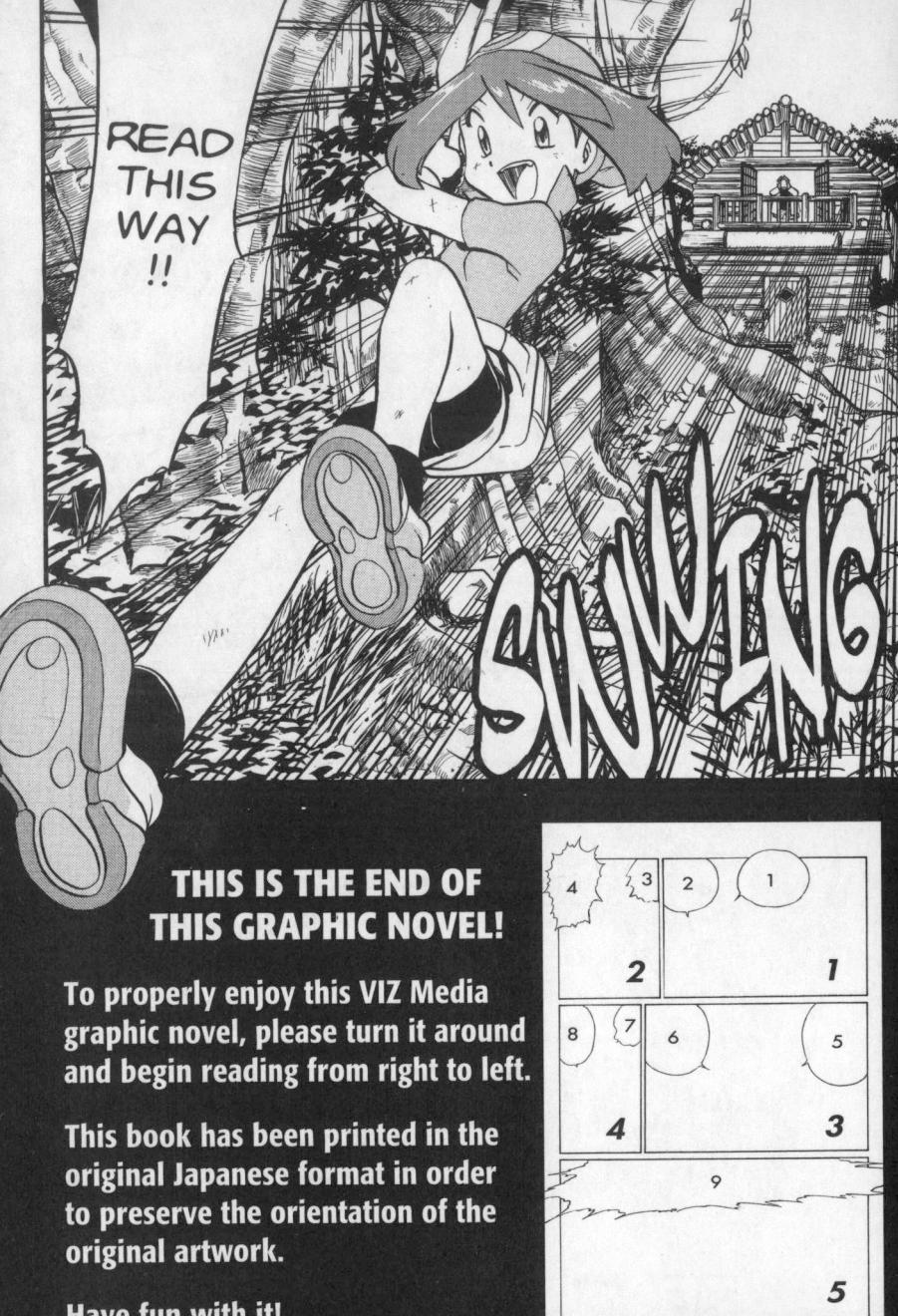

READ THIS WAY !!

SWWING

THIS IS THE END OF THIS GRAPHIC NOVEL!

To properly enjoy this VIZ Media graphic novel, please turn it around and begin reading from right to left.

This book has been printed in the original Japanese format in order to preserve the orientation of the original artwork.

Have fun with it!

FOLLOW THE ACTION THIS WAY. 142